CREATIVE
CONSPIRACY

CREATIVE CONSPIRACY

— THE —

NEW RULES *of* BREAKTHROUGH COLLABORATION

LEIGH THOMPSON

HARVARD BUSINESS REVIEW PRESS
BOSTON, MASSACHUSETTS

10 9 8 7 6 5 4 3 2 1

The web addresses referenced in this book were live and correct at the time of the book's publication but may be subject to change.

Library of Congress Cataloging-in-Publication Data

Thompson, Leigh L.

Creative conspiracy : the new rules of breakthrough collaboration / Leigh Thompson.
    p. cm.
 ISBN 978-1-4221-7334-3
 1. Teams in the workplace. 2. Creative ability in business. 3. Organizational behavior. I. Title.
 HD66.T477 2013
 658.4'022–dc23

                                        2012032811

The paper used in this publication meets the requirements of the American National Standard for Permanence of Paper for Publications and Documents in Libraries and Archives Z39.48-1992.

CONTENTS

ACKNOWLEDGMENTS

This book is lovingly dedicated to all the students who have graced my classes and courses at the Kellogg School of Management. Without those men and women and the organizations that encouraged and supported them on their journeys of self-development, I would not have a place in this world. The questions my students have raised and the personal stories of triumph—and sometimes disappointment—they have shared with me have shaped me as a scholar and profoundly affected decades of my research. Because of their insights, stories, and questions and their desire to improve their leadership and team effectiveness, I have a guiding purpose. And, with that purpose, I have joy in my life.

I solemnly caution my young PhD students—in training to be professors—that my litmus test for a new research project is: "Would I want to bring whatever results we might find into the management classroom?" This book is a compilation of the social science research I want to bring to the management classroom. Accordingly, this book contains highlights not only from my own research studies, but from those of my collaborators, colleagues, and the fields of management science, social psychology, organizational behavior, cognitive psychology, and developmental psychology.

The team who pulled this book together is the heartbeat of the Kellogg Team and Group Research Center (KTAG): Larissa Tripp, Joel Erickson, Marissa Greco, and Ellen Hampton. Their energy, dedication, and spirit embody the creative conspiracy this book is all about.

CREATIVE
CONSPIRACY

What Is a Creative Conspiracy?

Think about the most important project or task that is facing you at your job today. Ask yourself whether you are able to achieve your goal by working completely independently. If the answer is no, then list every single person you are depending on in some way—even if you have subordinates, you should list them and indicate how you depend on them. When I posed this question to several hundred people, no one said that they were completely independent. In fact, most people named at least three and sometimes one hundred people they rely on to achieve nearly anything.

Any time you cannot achieve your goals without the cooperation of others, you are collaborating. Collaborative teams realize that they are dependent on each other to achieve an important goal. *Collaboration* is the art and science of combining people's talents, skills, and knowledge to achieve a common goal. *Creative collaboration* is the ability of teams and their leaders to organize, motivate, and combine talent to generate new and useful ideas. Teams that conspire to commit creative and innovative acts are engaged in a *creative conspiracy*. When collaboration is conscious, planned, and shared with others, excitement builds and a conspiracy develops. The teams that can meet the creative challenges posed to them are the hallmark of the most successful organizations and the subject of this book, which contains state-of-the art research on collaboration and innovation.

In my research investigation of over one thousand team leaders spanning over fifteen years, 41 percent indicate that leading the creative team is of paramount importance. And the trend appears to be rising. As recently as ten years ago, only 39 percent mentioned creativity as a key leadership challenge; this rose to 47 percent since 2010. Yet although the result of some collaboration is greater than the sum of the parts, at other times, it falls far short. Of the different types of work that teams do, the creative aspect is the least understood, the most elusive, the most costly, and the one that managers and leaders most often unknowingly sabotage. Thus, understanding how to optimally structure the creative team for success is essential.

Unfortunately, there are a lot of unfounded beliefs about creativity. When businesses and teams operate using faulty myths about creativity and teams, they hold their teams back in their effectiveness. This book introduces an approach and easy-to-implement best practices for optimizing team creativity and collaboration. These practical strategies enable collaborative teams and their leaders to avoid the pitfalls that well-meaning teams often fall into and instead, capitalize on what actually works with regard to creative collaboration.

The *Group Versus Individual* Paradox

First, I need to warn you—there is a paradox that undergirds this book: although creative team collaboration is essential for companies and businesses, decades of research evidence clearly reveals that *groups are inferior to individuals* when it comes to creativity! Is there a solution to this paradox? I believe there is.

To illustrate this conundrum, I often challenge my clients and students with vexing teamwork simulations that require creative collaboration to succeed. However, the path to success is anything but obvious. Team members who are passive or overly controlling will certainly lead their teams to failure. Recently, I worked with a large group of executives and managers on collaboration skills. I divided them into four groups of about twenty-five people each. Each group was challenged to complete a twenty-five-minute task in which they needed to solve a "who-dunit" puzzle. I gave each member a written clue on a small sheet of paper. If they assembled all the clues and eliminated the wrong choices, they could easily reach the right answer. There was just one hitch: no one could write anything down, nor could they physically exchange the written clues. Rather, they had to talk, listen, and verbally communicate with each other. They were completely dependent on each other for success. Collaboration was essential.

One group simply gave up in frustration, convinced that the puzzle was impossible to solve. Another group persisted but got the wrong answer because of a faulty assumption. Yet another group disintegrated as the minutes ticked on, with various factions forming in the corners of room, arms folded, and a look of defeat on their faces.

Afterward, a young man in the group that gave up told me that his key takeaway from the exercise was that he never wanted to work in a team-based organization! He admitted that he was frustrated because no one approached the task in what he thought was a rational, organized fashion. He later confessed that all his life, he had been the guy that believed if you wanted something done right, you had to do it yourself. If there was a class project, he not only took the lead, he did everything. Depending upon other people really bothered him. This was the first time he really needed to rely on others for team success. Obviously, that is not the takeaway that I was hoping for.

Another group embraced the goal, chose a leader, and physically organized the information using their bodies as props and symbols. They pushed the limits by creatively using candy, coffee mugs, keys, masking tape, and pens as contraband props to organize the information. They manufactured printed words using pasted-together nametags. In short, they sneaked around me because they had created a conspiracy to succeed! To be successful, this challenge involves a lot of collaboration skills—listening, a balance of roles, and a creative, rule-bending mind-set.

This challenge is not unlike one that many real teams face—dependence on one another for success, frustration, lack of clarity, time pressure, and ambiguity. My independent-minded manager could not solve the puzzle alone; he needed to depend on the group. Yet in his mind, the group was dysfunctional. Most of the time, we are in a similar position in our teams.

In this book, I argue that collaboration is anything but intuitive and that merely assigning people to teams and telling them to be good team players in no sense sets the stage for effective collaboration. Companies need to disentangle true collaboration from simply physically being in the same place at the same time. *True collaboration often calls for periods of focused, independent work interspersed with periods of intense, structured team interaction.* In this sense, teams need to embrace dynamic, hybrid collaborative structures rather than static, monotonous structures.

When teams do work together face-to-face, they need to engage differently and not rely on gut intuition. This is where the myth-busting comes in. Collaborative teams need rules, they need conflict, they need some healthy self-interest, they need serious stretch goals, and they need to take much more control of the physical and social environment than most of us are accustomed to doing. Ultimately, creative collaboration is like a good party—people prepare individually, the leader-host sets a good stage, and people arrive in party mode, equipped with essential props. People don't show up hours early or too late, under- or overdressed, and with nothing in hand—nor do they stay too long.

This book is going to challenge your notions of what collaboration actually is. It is not 24/7 team cohabitation, it is not a long weekend retreat, and it is certainly not shared office space. Creative collaboration is characterized by thoughtful stage setting, complete with changes of scene, acts that open and close, and connection with the audience. It is not an anything-goes process. Unfortunately most organizations are not experts when it comes to creative collaboration; I'll start chapter 1 by exposing the most common myths about creative teamwork. I'll also reveal how to dispel faulty beliefs that give rise to ineffective strategies and introduce strategies and practices that will lead to creative success.

Setting the Stage for a Creative Conspiracy

While it might seem heretical to present data that teams are not nearly as creative as individuals in a book on creative collaboration, I can't ignore the scientific facts. Just as surely as cigarettes cause lung cancer, *groups are less creative than individuals*—at least when left to their own devices. Stated another way, when the stage has not been properly set for a creative conspiracy, groups will most assuredly underperform.

Some background explanation is in order here. To meaningfully compare groups and individuals, researchers have devised the perfect "control" group—the *nominal group*. A nominal group is a group of people who never actually interact. For example, say we wanted to compare whether a real, interactive group was more or less creative than the same number of people working independently. The people working independently are the nominal group. To make sure there would be no systematic bias in terms of the people in one configuration being smarter, younger, more attractive, or politically different than the other group, participants would be randomly assigned to work with a team or a nominal group. Hundreds of studies have been conducted using this very simple, yet very powerful design. In these studies, duplicate ideas created by the nominal groups are not counted. Furthermore, an independent panel of judges evaluates the output and the judges are "blind" with respect to whose ideas they are evaluating. And the findings? Virtually all of the studies unambiguously reveal that individuals outperform teams in terms of both quantity and quality.

When team members are working independently rather than together, there is obviously a much greater likelihood that they will duplicate one another's ideas. For this reason, teams and their organizations are often quick to criticize the wisdom of nominal teamwork. However, this concern may be overinflated or perhaps even a nonissue. Researchers Laura Kornish and Karl Ulrich measured undesirable repetition of ideas when teams generated ideas in parallel. In a substantial data set of over thirteen hundred opportunity spaces—ideas for an innovation that may have value after further investment of resources—they found little incidence of redundancy of ideas generated by aggregating parallel efforts, even in narrowly defined domains. Thus, this study suggests there is little reason to be concerned about team members working in parallel.

My point, however, is not that teams and individuals are mutually exclusive or should be pitted against each other, but rather that there needs to be an understanding of how teams and individuals operate and how individuals operate optimally within teams. By using hybrid, interactive meeting structures—characterized by periods of autonomous work punctuated by periods of intense collaborative work; clear goal setting and goal striving; a focus on quantity rather than quality; spirited and vigorous debating of ideas; and less talking and more doing, via brainwriting rather than brainstorming—teams can start reaching their creative potential.

A Word on What's in This Book and How to Use It

This book contains two things: (1) a lot of concrete examples of collaboration (the good, the bad, and the ugly) based on my colleagues' and my research and experience working with managers, leaders, and team members over sixteen years, as well as studies of creativity and teamwork conducted by the broader management science community; (2) a lot of prescriptive advice based on scientifically tested methods and strategies. Some of this will square with your intuition; much of it won't. This is partly because scientists don't do a good job of disseminating their research outside of the ivory tower. As a card-carrying member of the ivory tower, I see it as my duty to sift through the mass of research findings and bring the breakthroughs to the business world. Consequently, in this book, you will see some unsettling data and read about studies that suggest that we need to seriously rethink our creative team processes.

Besides the fact that, left to their own devices, teams are less creative than individuals, the body of research on collaboration has yielded many other surprising and counterintuitive findings, including:

- Teams that have "no rules" are less creative than those that have rules.

- Striving for quality results in less creativity than striving for quantity.

- Unstable membership enhances team creativity.

- Most companies cannot articulate, and routinely violate, the four cardinal rules of brainstorming.

- Most leaders cannot articulate the rules of brainstorming.

- Distrust can increase creative cognition.

- Thinking creatively leads to more dishonest behavior.

Some of the best practices I suggest might seem straightforward; however, some will be at odds with common wisdom. So, we will let the data decide. Bottom line: this book is heavily research based. I present empirical facts to support the best practices it outlines. This is what is known as *evidence-based management*. What does this mean exactly? Just like the hard sciences (e.g., chemistry, biology, genetics), the *data* should answer questions—not superstition, hearsay, or personal beliefs. In this regard, I encourage leaders and managers to treat their organizations like a scientific laboratory. Collect evidence. Do experiments. And choose best practices based on hard evidence. For example, in one of my courses, the managers were skeptical that groups are less creative than individuals. So, we designed an experiment in which we compared the creativity of managers, consultants, and investment bankers working alone versus in groups. We randomly assigned people to work alone or in groups. The individuals generated more ideas, and more unique ideas.

Before you are tempted to read this book cover to cover, consider doing the following:

1. Decide which chapter topic is most relevant to what you are struggling with this month, this week, and today with your team. Go directly to that chapter. For example, one of the leaders who we worked with was building a new team. The leader was concerned that group members establish a systematic way of providing feedback to one another, so he used a version of the peer feedback system presented in chapter 4 with his team.

2. After reading that chapter, make a personal commitment as to what is going to be different about your leadership going forward. Do at least one thing different today at work. Why? Active learning increases the likelihood of actually applying what we learn. People who learn passively (by watching others) are less creative than people who learn actively (by doing).

3. Then, have the resolve to announce your plan to the people you care most about. Tell them you are on a mission. And that you are open to accepting feedback.

4. Hand those people this book and ask if there is anything that they want to focus on—and tell them that you willing to collaborate with them.

By following these four steps, you have just engaged in the art and science of collaboration!

A Word About Me

When I joined the Kellogg School of Management in 1995, I was not experienced in executive education. So, during my first thirty days, I slyly inserted myself into an executive education classroom and seated myself in the last row, ready to take the pulse of the leaders and managers in the room. The fellow to the left of me apparently did not realize I was an undercover professor when he nudged me and said, "Do you think that anyone is going to actually use the stuff we are talking about in their company?" His innocent question launched me on a fifteen-year research program on knowledge transfer from the classroom to the real lives of managers, leaders, and executives. I made a pledge to myself that day to never do any research project unless I could bring the results back to the classroom and help managers and leaders derive meaningful best practices to use in their actual business situations.

Today, I am the director of the Leading High Impact Teams course and codirector of the Negotiation Strategies for Managers course at the Kellogg School of Management. I work with more than twenty-five hundred executives, leaders, and MBA students each year. They come from around the globe—Hong Kong, Germany, Israel, Latin America, Canada, and the United States. In any given week, I spend two to four days in the Kellogg executive center and engage in dozens of spirited conversations about the challenges of teamwork, creativity, conflict, and collaboration. It is these conversations that have shaped my research and this book.

When not in the classroom, I've conducted hundreds of research investigations inspired by the questions and dilemmas that managers bring to the classroom. The main thing I have learned from these managers is that leading teams is the most complex and the most important part of being a leader, and leading creative teams is challenging, risky, but ultimately the most rewarding. I've also learned that some of our intuitions about creative collaboration are valid, but many are not. Of all topics, creativity is the most elusive because our intuitions don't seem to square with the scientific studies. Consequently, the research questions I have investigated have focused primarily on collaboration, team creativity, learning, and win-win negotiation.

I should mention that when I'm not in the classroom, I am on my bike. I started training seriously in 2007 with the goal of doing local time trial races. Let me be honest—until 2007, I would have never referred to myself as an athlete. I certainly did not play any sports in high school or college. So my goal of becoming a bike racer at my age was somewhat preposterous. Once I did some local time trial races, I set my racing goals higher. In 2008, I won the USA Cycling Masters National Time Trial championship in my age category, and in 2010, I won the UCI World Masters Time Trial Championship in my age category. None of these things would have been possible without my coach, John Hughes, who set the stage for me through intense workouts that brought me to the point of physical and psychological failure, yet inspired me to keep training and collaborated with me on the building of a dream.

Until recently, I used to think that that cycling was a far stretch from the executive classroom. However, eventually the lightbulb went on for me, and I began to see the relationship between managers' work goals and their extracurricular goals. The managers who simultaneously want to be better parents, triathletes, and neighbors are also the ones who want to be better mentors and leaders in their own organizations. My coach helped me realize that no one ever achieves anything without three key things: (1) a clear goal; (2) passion; and (3) discipline. When you read this book, you will notice that it is extremely goal-focused and it will go deep in terms of exploring your passion and testing your discipline. The pace will be fast. The questions will be blunt. But I promise you will find strengths in yourself that you never imagined—just like I did on the bike and in the classroom.

Now, on to chapter 1, in which we'll debunk some common creativity myths—and where you'll do a Creative Collaboration Assessment to gauge your current team competence.

CHAPTER 1

Debunking Myths About Creativity

Several years ago, I made a research presentation to a group of scholars and a few consultants. My opening statement was, "Several decades of research have unambiguously found that teams are demonstrably inferior to individuals when it comes to brainstorming and idea generation." I thought that such a statement in the presence of academics would not cause too much commotion. I was wrong. One of the scholars was a lead consultant for a major Silicon Valley company that prided itself on creative idea generation, particularly in teams. This led to a spirited debate between the two of us that lasted through the evening and the next couple of months. I eventually dug up more than fifty peer-reviewed articles and put them on his desk. Every single article indicated that teams were inferior to individuals when it came to brainstorming.

I'd like to say I won the debate. However, companies do not want to stop brainstorming, even in the face of the evidence. Studies have included sophisticated methods for ruling out the effect of different personalities, differences in intelligence, and differences in industry experience. Further, the results have been replicated several, if not dozens of times and they show a clear causal pattern. To summarize succinctly in the words of organizational psychologist Adrian Furnham, professor of psychology at University College London, "The evidence from science suggests that business people must be insane to use brainstorming groups." But the research evidence—as powerful as it is—is not well disseminated.

When I work with clients, companies, and students, I find that they often operate with very specific beliefs about human creativity—some of which are correct. But many are wrong—at least according to scientific studies. In this chapter, I expose several of these key myths about creative teamwork. As you read, think about which of these myths is central to the way you work with your creative team and how you might better structure your team so as to capitalize on the strengths of the team members. Many of the messages in this chapter downright contradict common practice in organizations and even common sense. So I've been careful to provide data to back up these assertions.

Once upon a Time . . . Creativity Mythology

There is probably more mythology surrounding creativity than nearly any other topic in social science. Many companies have constructed fairy tales about what sparks human ideation that are completely misguided. Here are a few beliefs about creativity that have been endorsed by people in the business world. When you read these statements, think about whether you believe each is true or false.

1. Teams are more creative than individuals.

2. If you want to enhance creative teamwork, get rid of rules, guidelines, and norms.

3. Striving for *quality* is better than striving for *quantity*.

4. Active brainstorming is necessary to generate ideas.

5. Brainstorming teams should work closely together and tear down boundaries.

6. Team members should first brainstorm as a group to get the creative juices flowing, then work alone.

7. People who are pro-social (team-oriented) are more creative than those who are pro-self (individually oriented, or just downright selfish!).

8. Deactivating moods (e.g., peaceful reflection, relaxation, serenity) lead to more creativity than activating moods (e.g., anger, fear, happiness).

When Myth Becomes Pseudo-Science

If you are like most people, you have probably agreed with about 75 percent of the statements above. In fact, all of them are false. At this point, you may be ready to throw this book on the floor and get back to running your business. Before you do, pick the statement above that you hold closest to your heart and read the research. (I'll point to some of this.) You can test your creativity competence by reading the rest of this chapter, where we'll delve into each of the myths above—myths that have morphed to become pseudo-science in the business world—and which I do my best to debunk.

Myth #1: Teams are more creative than individuals.

As I touched on in the introduction, the assertion that groups are more creative than individuals has been scientifically tested more often than a great many claims in social science. We know that it is controversial to argue that teams are less creative than individuals. There is not a person who has ever been on a team who has not had the feeling or the experience that creative magic has indeed happened in their group. Yet, the data are painfully clear on this all-important question. So, why are so many teams and their companies under the powerful illusion that they are more creative? Well, for most of us, it just *feels good* to be part of a team, and so we think that magical things like creativity must be present when we are working with our team.

This myth of team creativity all began when an enterprising businessman named Alex Osborn published a book, *Applied Imagination*, in which he coined the term *brainstorming*. Osborn was a staunch believer in the power of teams. He was convinced that if teams did four simple things—express ideas openly, not criticize others, focus on quantity, and build on the ideas of others—they would easily outperform individuals. Apparently, this sage advice was enough for most organizations to adopt his belief and institute it into their best practices.

Sometime later, the academics asked for proof. Since Osborn did not have data, much less conduct controlled experiments, a flurry of research programs were launched on the question of whether teams or individuals were more creative. As I noted in the introduction, hundreds of studies were conducted that compared intact, face-to-face brainstorming teams with the same number of people—nominal groups—working completely independently. Nominal groups outperformed real groups in terms of quantity as well as quality.

Many executives and managers reject these ideas outright. But as previously observed, this is akin to dismissing the surgeon general's report that smoking causes cancer. In one recent simulation my colleagues and I conducted, the nominal groups generated over 20 percent more ideas and more than 42 percent more original ideas! It is nearly impossible to not get this effect.

The reason people think teams are more creative is that they believe in *synergy*. They believe that the whole is greater than the sum of the parts. But this does not appear to be the case—at least under typical conditions. It is certainly possible that synergy can take place in teams, but more often than not, it does not. For example, teams that build on each other's ideas don't create more ideas, and the ideas are not better.

What are the implications? Well, on nearly a daily basis, leaders and their companies make decisions as to whether to assign group projects or individual projects. This raises the question of whether we are efficiently using the talents of people in companies or whether we are falling far short of our potential by insisting that people work in groups when they might be well advised to work individually on a problem—at least for some period of time.

The solution, however, is not to dismantle teams, which are essential to reach organizational objectives. Rather, we need to rethink and restructure how teams work creatively. Left to their own devices, teams are usually poorly structured for the creative process. However, with a few key insights and simple best practices, teams can dramatically improve their performance and generate a creative conspiracy.

Myth #2: If you want to enhance creative teamwork, get rid of rules, guidelines, and norms.

Let's face it. Most adults don't like rules. We got fed up with them in grade school and looked forward to the day when no one would tell us what to do or when to do it. We embraced the idea that no rules freed our minds. Well, unfortunately, we were probably better off in grade school—or at least more creative in grade school. The data in this case are unambiguous. Groups that don't have rules or guidelines are distinctly less creative than those that have rules and guidelines.

How do we know? Paul Paulus and his team at University of Texas, Arlington, contrasted teams that followed guidelines with those that were set free to guide themselves. Teams with instructions and rules humbled the laissez-faire teams when it came to creative output.

There is also evidence that groups have difficulty functioning without rules. So, they often respond by making rules. For example, in one provocative field investigation, James Barker conducted a long-term study of the effects of removing rules and regulations in a team. The well-meaning CEO of ISE Communications made a commitment to restructure the organization into self-managing teams. Literally overnight, he reconfigured the physical workspace and created several work teams called Red,

Blue, Green, Orange, and so on. Before the change, three levels of managerial hierarchy existed between the vice president and the manufacturing workers. After the restructuring, the reporting rules were removed with the idea that this would empower workers and ideas. However, over the following four years, a curious thing happened: the teams spontaneously developed more rules similar to ISE's old bureaucratic structure (e.g., if you are more than five minutes late, you're docked a day's pay). The social rules were even more rigid. And workers nostalgically recalled the good old days of bureaucracy. Barker's groundbreaking study points to two simple truths about rules and creativity: first, removing rules in no way liberates people; and second, some rules are actually adaptive for groups.

The principle seems to hold for individuals, as well. Lilach Sagiv and colleagues compared how "intuitive" people and "systematic" people behaved under "structured" versus "free" conditions. Structured conditions involved presenting people with a form and challenging participants to find a creative way to use it; in contrast, others were given complete freedom to generate a creative form. Overall, creativity was higher under "structured" task conditions.

Myth #3: Striving for quality is better than striving for quantity.

We've been told all our lives by everyone—teachers, employers, friends, and family—that quality trumps quantity. To test this assumption, one study examined four different types of instructions: no stated goal, a quality goal, a quantity goal, as well as a joint quantity and quality goal. The results? Those who had the quantity goal generated more ideas and better ideas than any other goal.

What's the problem with focusing on quality to the exclusion of quantity? Several. First, quality requirements lead to *self-censoring*—people do not suggest ideas because they worry that the ideas don't meet the imposed quality criterion. They fear others will ridicule their ideas—this is known as *jeering*. We've all seen how this creates an uncomfortable silence and can also be demoralizing. So, people play it safe and don't say anything. Instead of ridiculing or badgering others, team members must find ways to stimulate and encourage others. Team members don't need to be criticized, rather they need ideas to stimulate the next idea, and so on. This is called *priming*: the act of stimulating new ideas and thoughts with a phrase, suggestion, picture, or idea. For example, the other day, I was facilitating a brainstorming session, and the group came to a grinding halt after about five minutes. With five more minutes left to work, they were at a loss for how to reinvigorate themselves. So we decided to look for inspiration in the environment. We raided briefcases and found various items—magazines, iPhones, personal photos, and so on—that the team spread out on the work table in front of them. Suddenly, new ideas started sprouting! Priming is like social popcorn—it stimulates others to suggest ideas.

A strict, or even loose, quality focus narrows the options. Quality requirements create smaller sets of ideas from which to choose. The smaller the set of ideas from which to develop and choose, the less likely it is that a truly great idea will emerge.

A related problem is the *primacy effect*: the strong tendency to be attracted to the first option that is suggested. There is a pervasive belief that the first idea is mission-critical for the creative enterprise—a misguided view of creativity that exaggerates the importance of the initial idea in developing a product. But Ed Catmull, president of Pixar and Walt Disney Animation Studios could not disagree more. According to Catmull, it is important to generate and sort through a mass of ideas—"it's like an archaeological dig where you don't know what you're looking for or whether you will even find anything. The process is downright scary." For that reason, I often try to get companies to avoid choosing the very first idea that is brainstormed.

Myth #4: Active brainstorming is necessary to generate ideas.

Idea exchange is a crucial part of creativity, and we sometimes lose sight of the fact that there are two key elements. First, people need to carefully process and understand the ideas in the group—this is known as *attention*. Second, they need to reflect on the ideas—this is known as *incubation*. *Incubation* refers to how our unconscious mind often works on a problem when we just can't think about it anymore. This is why sometimes people think of a solution to a problem when they are in the shower or taking a walk—they are not thinking consciously about a problem, but unconsciously, they are solving it. This is important, because incubation gets shut out by another dynamic that affects brainstorming—*fixation*. This is the tendency to focus on a limited number of domains or kinds of ideas. Fixation is thinking *inside* the box! Unfortunately, the very act of brainstorming with other people tends to lead to fixation, as compared with brainstorming independently. Indeed, over time, the quality, variety, novelty, and quantity of ideas starts to decline in a group. However, *taking a break* can stop this slide.

Engineers Paul Horowitz and Alan Huang were both facing extremely vexing problems concerning designs for laser telescope controls and laser computing. After struggling with the problem for months, they both visualized a solution in their sleep. Similarly, in the 1950s, Don Newman, a professor at the Massachusetts Institute of Technology was trying to solve a troublesome math problem. "I was . . . trying to get somewhere with it, and I couldn't and I couldn't and I couldn't." One night, he dreamed of the solution in his sleep and turned his dream into a published paper.

Studies of problem solving and incubation reveal that temporarily putting a problem aside and returning to it later can lead to more breakthroughs and superior performance than continuing to actively focus on the problem. Why? Steven Smith and Steven Blankenship of Texas A&M University argue in their *forgetting-fixation* hypothesis that correct solutions are made inaccessible during initial problem solving because we keep retrieving incorrect solutions. Thus, forgetting about a problem and focusing on something else can make correct (but dormant) solutions more accessible.

Myth #5: Brainstorming teams should work closely together
and tear down boundaries.

Private space and solitude are out of fashion. In some companies, requesting private space might even raise concerns about your teamwork ability or whether you are a "team player." Nearly all US workers spend significant time in teams, and 70 percent of us inhabit open-plan offices. Furthermore, in recent decades, the average amount of space allocated to each employee has shriveled—from five hundred square feet in the 1970s to two hundred square feet in 2010. When I went to primary school, our desks were in neat rows, and all my gear was loaded into my own space and sacks that hung on my desk; today, primary school classrooms are arranged in pods and rotated regularly. Yet, working physically close to others and removing all boundaries is in no way conducive to creativity.

Susan Cain notes in a 2012 *New York Times* article that Backbone Entertainment, a video game company in California, initially used an open-plan office, but soon realized that its game developers—the creative think tank of the organization—were not happy. So Backbone converted to cubicles, and those nooks and crannies soon allowed the game developers to think creatively.

Consultants Tom DeMarco and Timothy Lister studied the Coding War Games, a series of competitions that test software engineers' abilities, and compared the output of more than six hundred computer programmers at ninety-two companies. DeMarco and Lister discovered that the enormous performance gap between highly productive companies and less-productive companies was driven by how much privacy, personal workspace, and freedom from interruption that programmers had. Statistically, 62 percent of the best performers described their workspace as private, compared with only 19 percent of the worst performers. And 76 percent of the worst programmers said they were often "needlessly" interrupted, compared with only 38 percent of the best performers.

For all these reasons, the *cave-and-commons* workplace design may be ideal for team-based companies. In the cave-and-commons setup, people have common space to meet when needed and necessary, but they have their own private "caves" that they can retreat to for creative idea generation, which usually happens in solitude. This hybrid structure perfectly reflects the fact that the creative process is a fine orchestration of individual and group work. Let individuals think in their caves. Then let the team debate which of the ideas is the most valuable (this is when to bring the teams into the commons).

There is also a widely held related notion that the more time groups spend together, the more they will bond and perform well together. Think again. Karen Girotra, professor of technology and operations management at INSEAD, examined hybrid teams, in which individuals first worked independently and then together, and compared them with teams that worked only together. She found that hybrid structures led to more ideas, better ideas, and increased ability to discern the best-quality ideas.

Myth 6: Team members should first brainstorm as a group to get the creative juices flowing, then work alone.

People are under the mistaken impression that being in a group will supercharge idea generation and motivate them to think creatively. In fact, the opposite is true! It is nearly always better for people to work independently before moving into a group. Paul Paulus and his research team put this idea to the test by training people in several different modalities. Some people worked alone on a brainstorming problem and then moved into groups. Other people worked with groups and then moved to independent brainstorming.

The results were quite clear: those who worked independently before moving into groups had much better group brainstorming sessions! Why? The people who were alone initially in their own thoughts before moving into a team experienced much greater group creativity. When we are brainstorming alone, we are in a state of thought, not in a state of action. Conversely, when we work in teams, we start getting busy, making plans, and setting agendas—and this does not serve us well. By brainstorming alone first, the individual is not under the peer pressure of others. Moreover the individual does not have to pay attention to social cues or for that matter even listen to others. Rather, that person can think in a completely unfettered fashion.

Myth #7: People who are pro-social (team-oriented) are more creative than those who are pro-self (individually minded or just downright selfish!).

I warned you that some of the ideas in this book would not be politically or organizationally correct. This is one of them. For years, we've been told to act more like team players and put self-interest aside. In fact, that advice does not make sense for creative teamwork. People who are pro-self and have a high concern for their own interests are actually more creative than people who are pro-social.

How do you know if you are pro-self or pro-social? Well, as a start, do you resonate more with the statements like, "I enjoy being unique and different from others in many respects" or statements like, "Even when I strongly disagree with group members, I avoid an argument"? Are you more likely to state, "I do my own thing, regardless of what others think" or "It is important to maintain harmony within my own group"? What about, "I prefer to be direct and forthright when dealing with people I've just met" versus "I usually go along with what others want to do, even when I would rather do something different"? If you tended to agree with the first statement in each pair, chances are you are primarily pro-self. If you tended to agree with the second statement in each pair, chances are you are primarily pro-social. Don't misunderstand me—being pro-social is very advantageous in many, if not most, of life's situations. It is just not conducive to thinking creatively.

However, this book doesn't advocate creating a culture of self-centeredness. Rather, it points to ways of temporarily putting pro-social, communal concerns aside during a focused brainstorming session in order to activate or ignite a pro-self orientation for increased creativity. In my research with social psychologists Wendi Gardner at Northwestern University and Elizabeth Seeley at New York University, we've used a technique to temporarily engage pro-self views. To prompt people to be self-absorbed, we have them write or read statements that contain a lot of personal pronouns such as *I, me,* and *mine.* Conversely, to get people to focus on others, we have them read or write statements that contain pronouns such as *we, us,* and *ours.* We find that this simple mind exercise can temporarily activate either pro-self or pro-social concerns.

> *Myth #8: Calming, relaxing, peaceful deactivating moods lead to more creativity than activating moods.*

There is a widespread belief that creativity is best served through inner peace, serenity, and calmness. One of my colleagues was convinced that her own creative writing was best when she had no distractions, quietly sipping tea in a peaceful setting. However, after three months of such languid writing days, she produced nothing that she was proud of. Shortly thereafter, her first baby was born and her schedule went from long, open, peaceful, unstructured days to tightly orchestrated, minute-by-minute slots, punctuated by extreme activity. The result? She became prolifically productive. In her words, she was "wired." The way she put it to me was, "I have ninety minutes when Sam is napping, and I run to the computer and write like crazy. I'm totally focused." Turns out, my colleague is onto something. In fact, it is better to be aroused when attempting to think creatively.

In my research with Brian Lucas, we interviewed people about how they structure their environment when they want to be creative. Common responses included doing yoga, meditating, taking a nature walk, and looking at pleasant art. So, we put this to the test: we had some people listen to their favorite music, but we made others listen to a (boring) political speech. As you might expect, when people were listening to the speech, they became annoyed, frustrated, and agitated. Those listening to their favorite songs grew more relaxed and serene. We then examined their behavior in a creativity challenge and found that those who had listened to music dramatically underperformed in comparison with those who had been frustrated by the annoying political speeches!

Assess Your Team's Creative Know-How

Now that we've poked holes in some of the big myths surrounding creative collaboration, what can we do to make sure our own teams don't get ensnared by practices that limit their creativity? First, we need to set the stage by seeing where you are in terms of creative collaboration competence.

Think about the last meeting you had in which the task called for creativity. What did you do to set the stage? If you are like most people, you did not do anything different—or maybe you brought in the doughnuts! Most teams run every meeting the same way, no matter what the business at hand is. High-performance teams, however, constantly change gears so as to optimally meet the challenge of the day. If that challenge involves brain surgery or a SWAT mission, then clearly defined roles, top-down leadership, and a strong prevention focus (i.e., focus on what can go wrong and avoiding bad outcomes) is necessary. However, if the challenge of the day calls for brainstorming a new product idea or new ways of engaging customers, then the team must organize itself to be at its creative best, which will call for a different set of norms and behaviors. Establishing the ground rules that allow these norms and behaviors to occur is the part and parcel of the creative conspiracy.

Most people float into meetings and conference rooms that look strangely similar to one another, no matter what the true business at hand it. Why? In the Creative Collaboration Assessment that follows, we ask you to think about how your team conducts itself. Where do you meet? What are the spoken and unspoken rules of engagement? And how about these questions? Does anyone facilitate the meeting? Are any special props or materials brought in for the meeting? Are ground rules discussed? Sadly, most of the time, the answer is no, no, and not really. This suggests that leaders are not making most efficient use of their scarcest resource: people's time.

I developed a Creative Collaboration Assessment that invites you to examine your team's creative meetings—which, if your organization is like most, absorb at least 25 percent of your time, and often up to 50 percent or more. Once you have taken stock of just how you are using your own and other people's meeting time, turn to the scientifically tested best practices for optimizing the creative meeting contained in the assessment below. I suggest that you begin by completing the assessment yourself and then conduct an open-ended conversation among your team's members. Does everyone see the group's process in the same way? Where are the points of agreement? Disagreement? What works well in terms of your group's process? What does not work? What practices should be added? What processes should be abandoned? What needs modification?

The Creative Collaboration Assessment contains twenty items. As you consider them, imagine that a team psychologist is observing your team's every move through a one-way mirror. The psychologist is well trained and has studied thousands of teams. How would that psychologist describe your team? In short, take an objective look at your team.

The Creative Collaboration Assessment

1. With regard to ground rules and norms in our creativity sessions, my team . . .

    ☐ operates with dysfunctional rules and norms (0)
    ☐ really does not have any clear rules or norms (1)

☐ has knowledge of effective ground rules, but does not regularly use nor enforce them (2)

☐ regularly operates with at least the four cardinal rules of brainstorming (i.e., expressiveness, no evaluation, quantity focus, and building on ideas of others) (3)

☐ regularly operates with the four cardinal rules of brainstorming as well as additional rules that we have found to be particularly impactful (e.g., no storytelling, no explanations, encouraging those who are not making a contribution to contribute, etc.) (4)

2. With regard to conflict, my team . . .

☐ is not very nice; we engage in openly rude behavior— venting frustrations, jeering, personal attacks, and harsh criticism (0)

☐ is too nice; we actively avoid conflict (1)

☐ sometimes expresses conflict, but we try to separate the people from the problem (2)

☐ routinely engages in open, spirited debate, much as scientists do who hold different theories; we passionately attack the problem, but we respect our people (3)

3. With regard to a group facilitator, my team . . .

☐ has attempted to sabotage an outside (or inside) facilitator (0)

☐ has never used, nor is open to, using a facilitator (1)

☐ has used an untrained facilitator (2)

☐ has used a trained facilitator practiced in the art of creative teamwork (3)

4. In terms of external memory and recording aids (e.g., whiteboards, flip charts, cameras, videos, etc.) my team . . .

☐ meets in a room that is largely impoverished (no whiteboards, no flip charts, no note-taking, etc.) (0)

- ☐ meets in a room that has blackboards, flip charts, writing surfaces, etc.; we may occasionally use them but not regularly (1)
- ☐ actively uses the blackboards, flip charts, writing surfaces, in an attempt to memorialize ideas (2)
- ☐ in addition to actively using our space, we create a boneyard or repository of the ideas created that members can easily access before, during, or after meetings (3)

5. With regard to mental stimulation and things to keep us thinking, engaged, and invigorated, such as props, videos, games, primes, objects, pictures, stopwatches, toys, film clips, etc., my team . . .

- ☐ does not provide or encourage any kind of external stimuli such as pictures, toys, objects, etc. (0)
- ☐ has on occasion attempted to "liven up" our creative meetings through the use of props, humor, etc. (1)
- ☐ actively imports props, such as toys, devices, gadgets, as triggers for discussion (2)

6. With regard to mood, my team . . .

- ☐ looks like a bunch of grumpy men and women (0)
- ☐ is largely neutral (not happy, not sad—just there taking up space) (1)
- ☐ is often positive and upbeat (2)
- ☐ is consistently positive and upbeat (3)

7. With regard to goal setting, my team . . .

- ☐ has not set a goal as long as I can remember (0)
- ☐ sets safe/weak goals (1)
- ☐ sets definite goals (2)
- ☐ sets goals based on meaningful criteria and scientifically based benchmarks, and revisits those goals on a regular basis (3)

8. With regard to diversity, my team . . .

   ☐ has demographic or gender diversity that falls
   along fault lines (e.g., all women are in HR; men
   in engineering, etc.) (0)
   ☐ is largely homogeneous, with people having similar
   points of view, personality, and background training (1)
   ☐ has demographic and/or gender diversity that does not
   fall along fault lines (2)
   ☐ has deep-level diversity (based on skills, training,
   background, education) (3)

9. The size of my team is . . .

   ☐ unclear, since we have never specified who's on the
   team (0)
   ☐ consistently over 10 people (1)
   ☐ 8–10 people (2)
   ☐ 5–7 people (3)
   ☐ fewer than 5 people (4)

10. In terms of incentives, rewards, and consequences, the
    following best describes my team:

    ☐ many more sticks than carrots; underperformance
    more scrutinized than exceptional performance
    (punishment-focused) (0)
    ☐ no meaningful rewards or punishments
    (no consequences) (1)
    ☐ more carrots than sticks (reward-focused);
    exceptional performance noted more often than
    underperformance (2)
    ☐ meaningful process and outcome rewards (3)

11. The leader of my team is best described as . . .

    ☐ milquetoast: uninvolved and passive (0)
    ☐ transactional: gets the job done; acts like a manager (1)

☐ relational: nice, likeable, but not particularly strategic on tasks (1)

☐ transformational: consistently articulates goals and vision for the team (2)

12. If my team were having a brainstorming or creativity session, we would most likely . . .

☐ not do anything different than in any other meeting (0)

☐ hope that people share ideas (1)

☐ go around the table one by one and invite people to share ideas aloud (2)

☐ engage in brainwriting (the simultaneous writing of ideas) (3)

☐ engage in brainwriting for part of the time; and perhaps electronic brainstorming (4)

13. With regard to membership change on my team . . .

☐ there has been no membership change for five or more years (0)

☐ there has been no membership change for at least a year (1)

☐ new members have been added and some members have left in the past twelve months (2)

☐ we have planned membership change and rotation; and often invite people on a temporary basis (3)

14. With regard to office space, my team or company . . .

☐ is marked by closed doors and very few meeting spaces (0)

☐ has a largely, or completely open floor plan (1)

☐ is a careful balance of cave and commons, with private spaces and common meeting spaces (2)

15. With regard to time pressure in our brainstorming-creativity sessions . . .

    ☐ we meet for the same amount of time every week (0)
    ☐ we meet until we are finished (1)
    ☐ we strategically plan the length of the meeting and set goals (2)

16. The future-oriented mind-set of my team is largely . . .

    ☐ prevention-focused; the team worries about what can go wrong and attempts to avoid disaster or bad outcomes (0)
    ☐ promotion-focused; we focus on goals and think about success (1)

17. With regard to people skills (emotional intelligence skills) . . .

    ☐ plain and simple: my team does not have them (0)
    ☐ some members have people skills, but not everyone (1)
    ☐ several members have people skills and they coach others (2)
    ☐ the team has people skills; we actively coach each other, and the organization appreciates the value they bring (3)

18. With regard to free riders on our team (e.g., people not doing their share of the work, yet expecting credit) . . .

    ☐ free riders exist on our team and they get away with it (0)
    ☐ free riders exist on our team and we make weak attempts to confront them (1)
    ☐ we take proactive steps to discourage free riding (2)

19. In terms of outsiders, my team . . .

☐ does not trust them and does not involve them (0)
☐ may consult with them occasionally (1)
☐ regularly involves the input of outsiders (2)
☐ regularly involves the input of outsiders who are devil's advocates (3)

20. With regard to social networks, the members of my team are . . .

☐ disconnected from the rest of the organization (0)
☐ very closely connected to one another (1)
☐ closely connected to one another, yet have good working relationships with others outside of the team (2)

SCORING. After taking the Creative Collaboration Assessment, add up your answers across the twenty items. The points for each answer are in parentheses. Note that the minimum score is 0 and the maximum score is 55. We rarely see such extremes. An average score is around 28. The higher your overall score, the more creatively healthy your team is:

0–10 (Low): Scores this low should be an immediate call to action. Scores in this range are usually due to one of three things: (1) the team has not been taught the best practices of creative teamwork; (2) the team does not take the time or does not feel accountable for modifying the structure of the group; or (3) someone is actively sabotaging the team. The first two are easy to fix. Reading this book will undoubtedly improve your team score. Making even *one* change to your weekly team creativity meetings will have a marked effect on your creative output.

11–21: (Medium-low): You have much room to improve. We suggest focusing on two to three best practices to implement in your team. Be sure to introduce each practice by itself and build in new best practices incrementally. Ask for feedback and keep modifying.

22–32 (Average): This range is actually the danger zone because it is the zone of complacency. "We are OK. There is nothing to worry about. We are about average for our industry. Others are worse than us." If you find yourself in this range, make it a point to locate a team in your organization with a significantly higher score and invite them in for an informational session. Barrage them with questions. Ask whether it was worth it. (No doubt it was!). Find others in your team who are not satisfied with mediocrity and introduce one new best practice every month.

33–44 (Above average): Congratulations! Scores in this range are rare, and mean that someone on the team really is committed to the success of the team. Make sure you affirm this person's efforts. Ask how you can be an active contributor to the team's continual evolution. Celebrate your best practices. Offer to coach other teams.

45 and higher (Extremely advanced): You are a black belt creative conspirator. Because of you, your team is already functioning at an elite level. Find areas to continue to improve. Offer to coach other teams. Conduct smart experiments within the team to discover which practices had the biggest effect. Publish your findings and share with other teams in the organization.

A Look at What's Coming . . .

The guts of this book—the chapters that follow—speak closely to the questions on the Creative Collaboration Assessment. What's the bottom line on each one of the questions you just answered?

Here's a lineup of some of the key issues and themes I'll cover in the rest of the book, mapped to the chapters in which they'll appear.

- *Who needs ground rules?* It is a common fallacy to believe that creative teams should throw out all the rules. The right rules and norms actually liberate groups! However, not all rules are conducive for the creative conspiracy. The right brainstorming rules catalyze the creative effort and improve performance. The wrong rules lead to self-censoring behavior and frustration. Another problem is that teams often violate the very rules that they sought to put into place! I call this *team drift*—the tendency for organizations to slowly revert back to business as usual. This book is about staying on course and sometimes that means going into a headwind. This is why meeting facilitators are key. Chapter 7 provides a review of the original four rules of brainstorming and then supplements these with additional rules.

- *Conflict: can't live with it, can't live without it.* On the one hand, most people don't like conflict they seek to avoid it, and associate it with dysfunction. But teams that avoid conflict don't get a lot of creative work done. On the other hand, teams that embrace the wrong kind of conflict—engage in open confrontation, rudeness, or take-no-prisoners battle—have their own problems. Chapter 6 distinguishes two types of conflict in teams: conflict about the task (what should be done) and conflict about the people, often referred to as task conflict versus relationship conflict. The key is to be hard on the problem, not the people. This chapter teaches teams how to have a good fight.

- *The who and how of group facilitation.* Most team meetings are either facilitated by no one in particular or a leader who may have his or her own agenda. People who may not have group facilitation skills may do more harm than good. That's a waste of the group's time. It is important that someone take control of the process and engineer the meeting in a way to suit the goal. Creative teamwork is one type of work that teams do and setting the stage for creativity is anything but intuitive. Chapter 7 reviews the best practices for the creative conspiracy.

- *Aids, props, stimulation.* Somewhere along the line, someone decided that business meetings should be dull and people should not have fun. These same people decided that an eight-point font and a seventy-five-slide PowerPoint deck is also good for meetings. So most meetings take place with people seated around a table in a room with blank walls. Most people don't realize how much of their behavior and mood is affected by the environment, for example, by color. Seating behavior influences who emerges as a leader. Teams that have committed to the creative conspiracy carefully design their meeting spaces to invite and capture ideas. In Chapter 7, the challenge is how you would allocate a significant budget to organize the optimal creative retreat.

- *Mood.* Team leaders are extremely contagious. Mood is a temporary state that is either positive or negative and either high in energy or low in energy. Mood can be affected by a number of factors and mood strongly influences creativity. Chapter 5 discusses mood in detail and describes its role in motivating the creative team.

- *Goal setting.* Goal setting is hugely important for creative teamwork. Alex Osborn, the father of brainstorming, wisely realized that quality goals can stymie a team; in contrast, quantity goals liberate a team. Chapter 7 discusses the importance of setting stretch goals.

- *Diversity.* Diversity is like an onion, meaning that on a very superficial level, we might diversify, say, on skin or eye color or dress. On a deeper level, we might diversify on the basis of education and experience. And still deeper, there are differences in values and morals. There's a lot of evidence that diverse teams are more creative, but also experience more conflict. Chapter 3 takes up the question of diversity and how to build a heterogeneous team.

- *Team size.* Most team leaders make their teams too big, often by a factor of two or more! Consequently, meetings are often a waste of time, difficult to schedule, and hard to manage. As a general rule of thumb, I like Richard Hackman's advice: keep the team in single digits. I discuss team size in our chapter 3.

- *Incentives and rewards.* Incentives and rewards form part of the discussion in chapter 5, on how to motivate the team. Most people regard themselves to be intrinsically motivated but think others are in it simply for the money. This disconnect creates problems when we work with others.

- *Leadership.* Who should lead the creative team? Chapter 4 considers the characteristics of the ideal leader.

- *Brainstorming.* Brainstorming is such a common practice that there is scarcely an organization that does not purport to use it. However, most companies cannot articulate the rules of brainstorming, much less follow them. In chapter 7, the four cardinal rules of brainstorming are reviewed, along with the evidence that supports their effectiveness today. The chapter also reviews new research that further improves brainstorming effectiveness. It is imperative to structure the brainstorming session differently than other meetings. Failure to do so will mean that people may remain in the same passive-aggressive mind-set that they take into other meetings. Part of the creative conspiracy is to set the mood so that people are lured into engaging in thoughts and behaviors that, quite frankly, will not be appropriate in other contexts, but that will pave the road toward success in the creative context.

- *Team membership.* Teams that have masterminded the creative conspiracy are marked by high levels of efficiency and productivity, but there is also a special character to their boundaries and membership. They're very, very aware who's part of the team and who's not. They often have their own mystique—special names, inside jokes, and phrases that are usually not transparent to outsiders. However, nothing is forever and therefore, there is membership change in the creative team. The arrival of new members and departure of founder members instigates a self-reflective process in the team. Said simply, when people come and people go, that leads people to think about what the team is about. In chapter 7 I review some of my own research findings on the benefits of rotating team membership.

- *Where does the work get done?* The open floor plan was supposed to be a sign that we were team players and we could benefit more by socialization than by holing ourselves up. The open floor plan soon moved from the office space to the educational space. However, it just may not be the best thing for creativity. Groups who have crafted a creative conspiracy have private hideaways, and doors may be shut allowing individuals on the team to do what they need to do. Chapter 2 makes an argument for some degree of what might be viewed anti-social behavior in teams and chapter 7 focuses on the importance of hybrid meeting structures that balance team-time and alone-time.

- *Time pressure.* Is supposed to be bad, right? Lots of research suggests that groups simply work to fill their time. And whether teams meet for 1 hour, 90 minutes or 2 hours, there are no appreciable differences in group performance. Groups in the creative conspiracy meet without being bound by the meeting start and stop time. Chapter 7 presents evidence that as time pressure increases and the clock starts, creativity increases.

- *Social networks.* One interesting thing about creative conspiracies is that they often involve far-flung others. Thus, creative groups may very well not be pods of tightly knit friends; in fact, they may have little or no history of a working relationship. They are likely to be characterized as people who have disparate connections—clandestine ties to others who can help them. Chapter 3 focuses on how to compose the creative team and argues that odd bedfellows—as opposed to similarly minded buddies—make for the best creative teams.

⤙ Chapter Capstone

There are a lot of popular ideas on how to ignite creativity in teams. This chapter identified several plausible-sounding ideas that have gained popularity as best practices in organizational teams. These beliefs are so commonplace that they have achieved pseudo-scientific status. However, there is very little (or in some cases, absolutely no) scientific evidence to suggest that they work. In fact, some of these myths may even thwart creativity. The good news is that there are straightforward ways to fix most of the pernicious "best practices" that have crept into our organizations.

I hope this chapter has shaken the very foundations of how you think about creativity in your team. I've done my job if you are feeling somewhat rattled. Remember that complacency is the nemesis of the creative conspiracy. This chapter has challenged you to take a hard, critical look at the day-to-day practices of your creative team. If your score on the Creative Collaboration Assessment is low or lower than you desire, don't despair. There are several steps you can take to dramatically improve the creativity of your team. After all, that's the point of this book—to speak to the questions that the Creative Collaboration Assessment has raised and introduce the skills needed to spark a creative conspiracy. The next chapters introduce several best practices that are quite different than business as usual.

CHAPTER 2

Breaking Down the Barriers to Creative Collaboration

Somewhere along the line, we decided that being connected and social is a good thing. Conversely, doing things alone without the connection to others is just not fun, and in some cases, is deemed pathological. The pressure toward endless interaction has caused some of us to put our own desire for solitude on the back shelf. The modern workplace favors the gregarious, social worker who not only enjoys an open workspace, but is literally almost never alone. Susan Cain, author of *Quiet: The Power of Introverts in a World That Can't Stop Talking*, argues that loud-talking, brainstorming sessions favoring endless chatting are not serving us well. Thinking alone is hands down a better option—at least some of the time. Even extroverts produce better ideas when they are alone than when they are in a group. However, now that open-door policies, open-office floor plans, and the expectation that people should be reachable 24-7 have become ubiquitous, we have lost our solitude and, quite honestly, lost our mind—if that means the ability to think creatively.

Paradoxically, the rise of social media and the Internet has made people feel pretty lonely. Indeed, most Americans report having fewer close friends and confidants now than they did a generation ago. Sociologist Matthew Brashears at Cornell University surveyed two thousand adults and found that on average they had only two friends with whom they could discuss important matters—down from three in 1985. Millennials spend more time communicating with friends and social networks virtually than they do face-to-face. The frequency of virtual communication far surpasses that of all other types of traditional communication, such as phone calls and face-to-face socializing. Even though people consider it a status symbol to have five hundred or one thousand or even more Facebook friends, in truth, people who have a large group of acquaintances are *less* creative than those who have more close friends.

E-mail and other forms of virtual communication have created an organizational attention-deficit problem. Corporate employees receive and send an average total of 105 emails per working day, many of which are unnecessary. Indeed, the most productive and least stressed employees are those who don't check their mailboxes regularly. Some companies have had to introduce the e-mail vacation. In one study, information technology workers agreed to ignore work e-mails for five days, while others kept on reading and responding. Those who continued reading e-mails had more consistently elevated heart rates, while those taking the e-mail vacation had more natural heart rates, felt less stress, and were better able to stay on task. Productivity is not the only thing at risk. A study of forty-one thousand people found that those who never turn off their phones and computers are more likely to have sleeping disorders and suffer from depression and mental illness. Many of my clients and students have told me that there is an expectation that they are available 24-7 for their colleagues and customers and that the boundaries that used to exist between solo work and teamwork have all but disappeared—almost overnight—leaving most people feeling overwhelmed and unfocused.

In this chapter, I am going to make a decidedly antisocial argument that I think will ultimately spark more creativity within teams. I'll argue that we need to put up some barriers between people so that we can think and be creative when we are with them. I then address the question of just why it is that teams are less creative than individuals—a fact rooted in the dynamics of group behavior. And finally, I'll lay out ways we can realize our most creative self. Don't worry, I'm not going to suggest that everyone build a bunker or move into a lighthouse. But I will suggest that there is a time and place for social interaction and that it can be more meaningful when people have had the opportunity to engage in the necessary solo work that should precede group work. And that rather than being at the mercy of electronic media, we use it strategically.

I'll start by discussing some of the behavioral blocks that keep teams from being as creative as they could be:

- *Going with the crowd*: The largely unconscious tendency of people to change their behavior so as to win acceptance from others—in other words, conformity.

- *Riding the bus without paying the fare*: The tendency for people to not work as hard when they are in a group as they do when individually accountable for a project, also known as *free riding*.

- *Team superiority complex*: The tendency to think *95 percent of us are in the top quartile*—in other words, that one's own group has been more productive in a meeting than is actually warranted.

- *The tyranny of the average*: The tendency of groups to regress toward an average, whether that be an opinion, design, or even a group performance effort.

- *Cognitus interruptus*: The tendency to multitask in groups, even though no one is good at it and the group ends up neither listening nor performing very well.

- *Dumbing down*: The fact that people are obsessively concerned with what others think of them and thus play it safe by being passive and often not doing anything extraordinary so they won't attract attention.

Going with the Crowd

Whether we want to admit it or not, we are conformist creatures. Any time we bring our behavior into alignment with others and their expectations, we are conforming. Any time we change our behavior because of the presence of others, we are conforming. Most of the time, this makes a lot of sense—after all, if we did not conform to the rules of traffic lights, we would crash our cars into one another. Or think of the consequences if we did not observe the conventions of standing in queues or participating in business meetings! Most of the time, things work better when we conform to protocol and fall into line. And in most cases, conformity acts as a social lubricant. Things go better when people adapt to and make room for each other. The one notable exception is the creative process!

As humans, we are hardwired to conform and so we modify our behavior, our speech, and even our unconscious thoughts in an effort to fit in. Psychologically, there are two major reasons why people conform—they want to be liked and they want to be right. In other words, we sometimes conform because we know that others will like us more if we agree with them. There is a lot of scientific evidence that backs this up. People treat nonconformists pretty badly. Psychologist Stanley Schachter studied how groups treat deviants—people who simply hold different opinions than the rest of the group members. He found that such people are the target of extraordinary criticism and group pressure. When a group member takes a different view, the group begins by trying to persuade that team member to change his or her mind. When that does not work, they often escalate their criticism and even express dislike of the deviant. Eventually, the group ostracizes the deviant.

We also conform because we figure that there is wisdom in the crowd. In short, when we are uncertain about how to act, feel, or behave, we naturally look to see what others are doing. For example, suppose you are attending your first underground dinner party. You have been sent a secret password and location a few days in advance, but that is all you know. You are unsure of what to expect so you play it safe when you arrive by barely mingling. By observing others and following suit, you quickly learn that there is no assigned seating and that you should absolutely not ask to see the kitchen, or heaven forbid, ask for any substitutions, even if you have a food allergy—in short, you conform! Conformity is a type of vicarious learning.

Most of the time, we conform unconsciously. We don't even have to think about the fact that we are monitoring others and adapting to them. For example, many people start to dress like their boss, although they don't realize it. Even more often, people unconsciously mirror their boss's nonverbal behaviors during a meeting—using similar hand gestures or crossing the same leg, and so on. This is not crazy behavior. Indeed, there does appear to be an evolutionary advantage for those who mirror. People who dress like their boss actually get paid more and promoted more quickly. When we mirror others, they like us more. Unfortunately, the downside is that we behave in a more conformist fashion.

However, brainstorming demands nonconformist behavior. When we are in a brainstorming meeting, we need to check conformity at the door. Diversity of thought and mind is key for the creative thinking process. This is hard to maintain, though, because we don't realize how much conformity pressure affects us. Over time, as members conform to one another, they become distinctly *more* homogeneous. In one investigation, people were given a free association test in which words were flashed on a screen and participants were asked to say the first thing that came to mind. People who were in the presence of others took longer to respond—suggesting that they were mentally editing their responses. And their verbal responses were more clichéd and typical. In contrast, people responding by themselves were faster and they made more unique, nontraditional responses.

The following conditions tend to heighten our own tendency to conform:

- When people feel incompetent or insecure about their knowledge or talent

- When the group has a minimum of three people

- When the rest of the group is unanimous

- When a person admires and likes the group

- When a person has not previously made a public commitment to a point of view

Undoing Conformity

I'm not suggesting that people in groups should become rabid nonconformists. Most of the time, conformity provides the social lubrication that allows people to work together in a harmonious fashion. What I am suggesting, however, is that when we launch a brainstorming session, we put aside conformity norms and act as independently as possible. One study examined how conformity pressure affected the creative output of teams and found that it is generally not effective, except in cases of people who lack creative talent. Specifically, I suggest that leaders and facilitators begin a brainstorming meeting by clearly stating something like:

> Look, we're all colleagues here, and we want to have a productive meeting. However, to really achieve the goals of this brainstorming session, we need to stir up some outrageous ideas and set all questions of feasibility, practicality, and, for that matter, political correctness aside. Believe me, there will be plenty of time to evaluate and rule out ideas, but I want to personally encourage the outlandish this afternoon. And, if we start to stray back to everyday rationality, I'm going to bang this gong [or drum], and you can too!

In my coaching work with leaders and their teams, I encourage leaders to bring in a strange and noisy prop, such as a gong, bell, drum, or even water gun, so as to set the stage for a very different experience. Another favorite technique of mine is to give the team five minutes to talk about their most embarrassing experience in the past year—they often quickly let their guard down. Similarly, when comedians or improvisational actors warm up for a scene, they often do something that is embarrassing or self-revealing. For example, they talk about the most embarrassing part of their body or make gaseous sounds—it is a way to take down their guard.

Riding the Bus Without Paying the Fare

One of the most pernicious problems in almost any team endeavor is the fact that some people do not contribute as much as others to the group's effort. Yet they still enjoy the benefits of being part of the team. Free riding is the number-one complaint among people who work in team-based organizations. All of us have had the unpleasant experience of being in a group in which some people fail to do their share of the work, do crummy work, don't follow up, don't even show up—and then have the gall to include their name on the report or project or to reap the financial rewards!

Economists coined the term *free riding* to explain why people do not contribute their fair share in groups. For example, just over 1 percent of the population voluntarily supports public radio and public TV in the United States. Another example: in the United States, tipping at restaurants is completely voluntary. Parties of two, three, and four often leave pretty good tips. However, as the number of people in the party increases, the percentage of the tip decreases. Restaurants and waitstaff are onto this, which is why restaurants often add a mandatory 15 percent tip to the bill for parties of six or more. As it turns out, people in groups are more likely to want to take a free ride—enjoy the benefits of wine and food and company without paying for it. You may have heard of the *bystander effect*, or the tendency for people to not help a crime victim or someone in need. Well the effect is stronger as the number of bystanders increases.

Free riding also explains why some people consume more than their fair share. For example, as the size of a team increases, people become more selfish in situations in which they must exercise personal restraint. They eat more, take more tokens, and grab more swag when they're in the presence of others. Researchers have long known that in both animals and adults, consumption of food increases as the number eating increases. The same holds true for children. In one study, when preschoolers ate graham crackers in groups of three or nine, the children in the larger group ate 30 percent more.

In short, free riding is just like what it sounds like. It is the tendency for people to enjoy the benefits of being in a group but do less of the work, contribute less, or take more benefit than would actually be fair. People are remarkably clever when it comes to free riding. And they don't look at their own behavior as being self-interested. Rather, they justify it. My colleague Dave Messick set up a work-for-pay simulation in which people could work at a small task—grading exams—and then get paid. There was a strong tendency for people to take advantage of the situation by focusing on whatever aspect of the task they did best—and thus overpay themselves. People who worked longer hours believed they deserved more pay; but those who had actually graded more exams (in less time) believed that they deserved greater pay.

Free riding plays out at work, too. Chances are, you have been a member of a study group or work team in which a minority of people are doing most of the work, while other team members are enjoying the benefits. Just how pervasive is the free-rider problem? A meta-analysis of seventy-eight studies demonstrates that free riding is robust and generalizes across tasks and populations. Whether the task is shouting, hand-clapping, paperwork, oral presentations, brainstorming, writing reports, or pure physical labor, people work noticeably less hard in the presence of others than they do alone. There are many reasons why free riders show up in groups. First and foremost is the desire to benefit. In addition, free riders may believe that their own efforts are dispensable and not necessary for the group's success.

Every term when I teach my classes, I have a similar experience: halfway through the term, a group of students visits my office to tell me that there is one person on their team who is not pulling his or her weight—not contributing to the group project, which has a significant negative impact on their grades. By the time this group visits me, they are frustrated and at the end of their rope. I ask them what they have done to address the problem and usually get a mixed set of responses. Some groups have not taken any action because they fear that any kind of confrontation will only make things worse, and so the problem perpetuates. Other groups hinted at the problem, but the team member in question did not get the hint. Other groups have taken rather drastic measures and have ousted the nonperforming team member in question. I don't like any of these approaches.

But there has to be an approach, because free riders don't just stir up resentment among the contributing members—they negatively affect the performance and creativity of the whole team. Take the case of Chris. Chris is a perfectly polite guy and quite friendly. When he first began to show up late for meetings, the rest of the team did not say anything, and even made light of the situation. Chris took the absence of criticism as an OK to skip out on further meetings. When I suggested that the team confront Chris or at least talk with him, the members were reluctant. They somehow thought this was somebody else's job or that the situation would somehow resolve itself. It did not. In fact, it got worse. I made the suggestion again, but the team assumed that talking would not make a difference. So the team members began to disengage from the team mission; not long afterward, the entire team slipped into mediocrity.

To make matters worse, the free rider is often blissfully unaware of the fact that he is not pulling his weight. The rest of the team grows resentful and this creates a negative "doom loop."

So, is free riding inevitable? No. It is not always the case that the presence of other people causes some or all people in a group to work less hard. In fact, three possible outcomes may result when people are in the presence of others:

- *Free riding or social loafing*: Occurs, as we've learned, when people in a group work less hard than they would individually. The group member may falsely believe she is contributing or, conversely, may know that she is shirking, but has an incentive to benefit from the group's work. *Example*: In a group of managers working on a complex consulting engagement with firm deadlines and deliverables, one or two people are doing most of the work, while others continue to be compensated for their time and praised by the client.

- *Social matching*: Occurs when people in a group attempt to match their performance or rate of productivity to what others are doing. This illustrates a tendency for people in groups to converge on a group average. *Example*: A new salesperson in a technology group learns of the average sales quotas produced by other colleagues and attempts to match those.

- *Social competition*: Occurs when people in a group work harder in the presence of others than they do working alone. For example, joggers speed up their pace when they're with others, cyclists ride faster when others are around them, and some Olympic athletes make their best times when competing against their archrivals.

Ideally, we would like social competition to occur—provided that the competition is healthy and constructive. But that doesn't always happen, even when attempts are made to stimulate competition. One study examined how giving group members public information about the performance of others affected their behavior. Instead of competition, there was a strong tendency for group members to engage in social matching.

What to Do About Free Riders?

Team leaders often unwittingly create conditions for free riding to occur in teams. How can leaders set the stage to minimize the likelihood that free riders will pervade the group? It is important to be proactive about free riding before the team sets off to work. Consider one or more of the following practices.

DON'T MAKE THE TEAM TOO BIG. Free riders often experience *diffusion of responsibility*—in short, they don't feel personally accountable for performing because there are others who can do the job. Consequently, the larger the team, the less likely it is that any given member will work hard. This is why small, diverse teams are ideal. A good rule of thumb is: don't put people on the team unless there is a good reason. (We discuss team size more in the next chapter.)

ASSIGN ROLES. Teams in which members have clear roles and responsibilities are less likely to harbor free riders. Conversely, when members are assigned special, meaningful tasks, they are less likely to loaf.

STRENGTHEN TEAM COHESION. People who are more identified with their team are less likely to shirk. In exercises in which people are tempted to be selfish rather than cooperate with a group and potentially be exploited, people are much more likely to cooperate if they perceive themselves to be similar to others. One example of perceived similarity? Wearing similar t-shirts while focusing on a shared goal. Similarly, studies of cooperation in online interaction, in which people are not face-to-face, reveal that even using the same lingo, such as "lol," increases similarity! When people using Instant Messenger (IM) employed the same linguistic terms or adapted or matched to their contact's linguistic terms—for example, using the European term *soccer* instead of the American term *football*—they collaborated more. When less similar linguistic terms were used, people tended to focus more on personal gain and less on collaboration.

Similarly, teams that talk about what they have in common are less likely to free ride than those that talk about their differences. In short, focusing on their collective identity, rather than individual identities, increases cooperation and decreases free riding. One executive student of mine was poised for an aggressive, contentious negotiation that was headed for mutual disaster, but when he discovered that the key negotiator on the other side had been a graduate of his own alma mater, the tide turned and a win-win agreement was forged. This also explains why people from collectivist cultures are less likely to free ride.

However, if you want to increase divergent, creative thinking, make sure you do not create too much homogeneity. Creative, divergent tasks are best accomplished by groups that value individualism and uniqueness.

CRAFT A TEAM CHARTER. A team charter is a living document, written by all team members, specifying the mission of the team and the expectations they hold of one another. People are much less likely to renege on an agreement that they have agreed to in writing.

MAKE TEAM MEMBERS IDENTIFIABLE. Free riders often get away with murder because they can hide in a crowd. When team members believe they are identifiable or personally accountable for their performance, free riding is less likely. In one experiment, my colleagues and I had groups engage in a brainstorming task. However, we added an unusual twist: we placed a tape recorder on the middle of the table in half of the groups. The other half of the groups did not have a tape recorder on the table. We told the groups that we *might* want to know who said what after the brainstorming session. Even though we never listened to the tapes, the groups that *thought* that their ideas were identifiable outperformed the groups that were not recorded.

PROVIDE TEAM PERFORMANCE REVIEWS AND FEEDBACK. Because free riders are often blissfully unaware that they are not contributing as much as they should, it is important to provide feedback about their behavior. I use a dialogue-based peer review that involves four steps.

1. *Generating feedback*: Every team member writes three pieces of positive and three pieces of developmental feedback for every member of the team. Initially, people will resist and make plausible-sounding excuses, such as, "I really don't have anything to say . . . that is negative."

I simply respond that each team member is a work in progress and it is our responsibility to help one another on our journey to improve. I don't use the terms *negative feedback* or *critical feedback*; I call this type of feedback *developmental feedback*.

2. *Anticipating feedback*: I always ask members to anticipate the feedback that they will receive. When they have received the feedback (step 3), I ask members to make a note of what they expected to hear and what is surprising. All of this is done in a team setting, with members summarizing their expectations and noting the information that is confirming as well as the information that is surprising.

3. *Delivering feedback*: Once I have collected all the positive and developmental feedback for each member, I assemble it and give the individual team members their feedback with the strict understanding that no one should attempt to guess who made the comments. I usually type the comments and put them in individual envelopes for members.

4. *Learning from feedback*: As a final step, each member is expected to prepare a personal development plan. This is where the rest of the group can be helpful and make suggestions as to what could be acted on and how.

Why construct a qualitative, dialogue-based peer feedback system like the above rather than simply a system in which people get numeric scores? First, we learn more from dialogue than from numbers alone. Second, no one is singled out because everyone goes through the same process. Everyone receives feedback from everybody else—and most important, everyone receives an equal balance of positive and developmental feedback. Asking members to anticipate their feedback encourages self-reflection. It is worth noting that self-evaluation does not increase creativity unless people feel that they can improve. Asking team members to propose a personal development plan assures that the information is followed by action.

I Tried All the Above Stuff and I've Still Got a Problem

Once a free-riding problem has emerged, the team and the team leader need to take action. The key is to do three things: (1) raise awareness (often the free rider is unaware that his or her contributions are falling short of expectations; (2) get the team member to commit to change his or her behavior; (3) plan a follow-up to assess whether the behavior has changed. To make this even more concrete, team leaders can take the following actions.

First, the team leader should tell the group that she will be speaking to all members individually concerning the issue of workload and contributions. This does two things: (a) makes the free-riding problem a group issue and (b) indicates that no one is being singled out.

Second, the team leader needs to hold those discussions, being careful to follow a similar protocol with each team member. I suggest questions such as, "What is your assessment of the contributions and workload in this group?" "If you had 100 points to assign to reflect the contributions each person is making, how many points would you give to yourself? Others?" It is very important that the team leader share her evaluation of that team member's contributions. If that person is one of the free riders, the team leader should say something like, "My personal assessment is that you are not contributing as much as others. I would like to know whether my observation surprises you or is consistent with your own perception. And then I would like to discuss how we might change that."

The free rider will often either deny or, more commonly, make excuses for this behavior. The team leader should persist with the discussion of how the team member could modify his or her behavior and should express confidence in the team member's ability and willingness to change. Finally, the team leader should ask for a commitment from the team member; for example, "Can I have your word that you will, as of this point, do x?" The team leader should ask every team member for his or her personal assessment and action plan in writing.

Third, the team leader should schedule a follow-up meeting with each team member to provide feedback on what has been learned during this period and to see whether things are improving. The key is to make the free rider an active participant in the change process.

If these steps don't work, then I suggest that the team leader schedule one more meeting with the free rider in which she provides a review of when the problem was first noticed, recaps all the ensuing conversations, and simply announces that the problem will no longer be tolerated. The team leader can tell the team member that she has reached a conclusion that was not easy to reach, but necessary. The leader should pause at this point and ask if the team member knows where this conversation is going. More than 50 percent of the time, the team member will simply finish the sentence by saying, "So, I'm off the team?" The leader should nod and say, "That is correct."

Team Superiority Complex

"Ninety-five percent of us are in the top quartile." That statement is just logically impossible. Yet most people regard themselves as above average on everything from driving ability to nonverbal acuity. The same is true for their groups. Most people think their team's performance is most assuredly above average. And most people believe that they perform better in a group than they do individually. This is called the *illusion of group productivity*. It's the unfounded belief held by millions of people that our groups are more productive and are more creative than they actually are. Research has clearly shown, however, that this is dead wrong. Groups are distinctly less productive than individuals when it comes to creative performance. You might wonder how millions could be wrong. The answer is that we are social animals—people *like* being in groups. It feels good to be around others. Our mood improves. In short, teams have an inflated sense of their own productivity primarily because they have enjoyed being in the group and being in a group feels good.

However, this does not mean groups are more creative. Nevertheless, people cling to the illusion of group productivity. For example, people who have been part of a brainstorming group session *believe* they have generated more ideas than individuals who have brainstormed alone. However, these brainstorming groups are only about half as productive as an equal number of individuals brainstorming alone.

What can you do to avoid falling victim to the illusion of productivity? Try these three steps:

1. First, be clear about the mission of the group: *Yes, we want to have fun, but we also want to accomplish some real work*. Commit at the outset to a clear stretch goal.

2. Second, think about having three distinct phases to your group meeting: a beginning, a middle, and a close. The beginning should be social time. Because we are social animals, we have a distinct need to socialize and bond, so recognize that and set time aside for that to occur. I recommend around five to ten minutes, maximum. Then at the appropriate time, roll up your sleeves and begin the process of conducting the actual work of the meeting.

3. Finally, set aside three to five minutes to close the meeting. Ask the following questions: What worked well/not so well about our process? How is our output? What can we do to improve both?

The Tyranny of the Average

Most people seem to intuitively understand that others in a group don't want them to stand out in a way that might bring unwanted attention to the group as a whole. At the Chicago Hawthorne Electric company plant, workers on the line experienced a curious group phenomenon: they got "binged"! When one line worker felt that another was working too hard or not working hard enough, that overperforming or underperforming worker got smacked sharp and hard on their upper arm—a physical attack called *binging*. To the binged worker, the message from the group was clear: "Don't stand out." The group did not want free riders, but they also did not tolerate *rate-busters*—the name given to those who worked harder than the rest of the group and sent the message to management, *"Well, if one of us is working this hard, then it is reasonable to expect others to work hard as well."* Even though binging (or other physical intimidation) is rarely reported these days, workers have devised other ways of signaling to their colleagues just what is expected of them. In one nursing home, a new nurse's aide found herself accused of rate-busting when she fetched coffee from a downstairs cafeteria for a resident. A fellow aide confronted her, telling her that she couldn't do that because she (the veteran) wouldn't want to have to do the same: "Just tell [the patient] no," she added.

Regression toward the mean is the tendency for a given person's behavior to converge toward an average. On an individual level, each one of us has a "normal" or "set point" on just about anything that we aspire to do. For example, suppose that you take a standardized test and get a rather low score. You study and take the test again, and your score improves dramatically. However, when you take it a third time, your score gets lower. Regression toward the mean also explains why athletes cannot get a personal best every time they train, much less perform. Certainly, athletes, students, and executives all want to get better, but after a while it is hard to show consistent, steady improvement.

Groups, as we have seen, easily fall victim to the *tyranny of the average*—a strong tendency for people to establish norms and for groups to converge to those norms. This is clearly not conducive for breakthrough performance. But it gets worse. There is a tendency for the lowest performers to pull down the average of the team. What this means is that a low-performing team member might cause an otherwise high-performing team member to be worse. Why would this be the case? As an example, consider a group of salespeople whose sales are tracked on a daily—sometimes even hourly—basis. Anyone in the group can quickly see how much product others on the team have sold that day. When this group initially forms, there might be large differences in individual sales performance, with some being particularly high performers and some significantly less productive. Over time, however, they tend to converge toward a group average that is usually lower than the simple arithmetic mean of what their individual sales are. Why? Well, for one thing, a high-performer may simply stop working so hard. He may think to himself, "Why should I bust my butt trying to work hard if my team is not performing at my level?" Moreover, people are more likely to harm a higher-performing team member by interfering with their work, getting into arguments, and gossiping about them—particularly when they feel they cannot perform at that level. Finally, it is harder for a low performer to start performing at a higher level than for a high performer to start performing at a lower level. It takes motivation and skill to improve performance. Bottom line: the productivity levels of people around us have a powerful norming effect on our own performance.

The tyranny of the average is yet another reason to think carefully about whom to put on a team. It also suggests that there is some truth to the adage that one bad apple can spoil the whole bunch. Think of it this way: in general, it is not considered desirable to be too different from other group members. In a brainstorming task, group members may not want to outperform their fellow team members. Accordingly, low-productivity people may attempt to increase their output so as not to appear incompetent or unmotivated. Yet low-productivity people may simply not be able to perform much better, and so there is a competency ceiling. Conversely, high-productivity people may decrease their output because they don't want to do all the work and let others ride free. As this suggests, and research has shown, the difference in the sheer volume of ideas generated by people is lower for interactive groups than for nominal groups. And, more sobering, in the interactive groups, the partner with the higher rate of output attempts to match the partner with the lower output more than the reverse.

Regressing to the Mean? Or Raising the Bar?

In sum, several investigations have found evidence for performance-matching in creative teams. Not surprisingly, there is more of a group-averaging tendency in interactive groups than in nominal groups: the performance of people who are in interactive groups is more similar than the performance of those in nominal groups. More notably, researchers have found that groups often settle on a level of performance early on and don't change it over time. For example, the performance of a group in their initial session predicted their performance on a different problem two sessions later.

Yet is it always the case that teams converge toward a group average? Are there ever cases where teams will attempt to reach a new level set by a high-performing group member? A quite different view of performance matching is that groups stimulate *competition* or *raising the bar*. Simply stated, people in a team might challenge one another to perform better. For example, in one investigation, the productivity gap between interactive and nominal groups was eliminated when the interactive groups were given a performance standard comparable to that of the typical performance of nominal groups. Thus pressure from outside a group—in the form of information about the performance of others—might be effective in spurring competition; and when some degree of competition is introduced in the group, people are motivated to match the performance of the best group members.

Thus, my best advice on how to raise the bar rather than regress to the mean is to take the focus off intra-team comparisons and instead focus on comparing one's team to a model team or yes, perhaps even a rival team—because when people compare themselves to others, they improve their performance and they are more creative.

Cognitus Interruptus

Do you know that it takes the average person seven minutes to regain focus after he or she has been interrupted? Think about it. Every time you check your e-mail when it pings, it takes seven minutes to get back on track. Do you also know that fewer than 95 percent of adults are able to multitask effectively? The rest of us are downright multitasking failures.

Unfortunately, the problem is that we are not aware that we are easily distracted and don't multitask well. *Cognitus interruptus* is the term I use to refer to the fact that when we're in a group, or even logged into a computer, we must battle constantly to keep our focus of attention. In a study conducted at the University of California at Irvine, it was found that when someone is interrupted, the person does not resume to the original task until two other activities are completed.

Being in a group involves a complex symphony of skills: people have to listen, speak, regulate taking turns, show appropriate nonverbal behaviors, and sometimes—heaven forbid—take notes or summarize. In short, whenever we are in a group, we are usually multitasking, not the least of which involves listening and speaking. Have you ever noticed how people at meetings compete for attention and floor time? Sometimes they jiggle in their chair just before they want to speak, or draw a loud breath, or clear their throat. Sometimes they are successful, other times others simply ignore them and take the floor themselves. One of the major reasons why groups are less productive than individuals when it comes to creative thought generation, or *ideation*, is that they are simultaneously competing for the floor. *Production blocking* refers to the kind of interference people in groups encounter when more than one person is trying to speak at the same time. The mere act of "taking turns" to express ideas severely curtails the volume of ideas that a group can generate. It is not surprising that the production-blocking problem grows exponentially as the size of the group increases; two people experience a rather small level of production blocking (10 percent), but a group of four suffers a 25 percent reduction in productivity!

Production blocking refers to the time wasted while group members "queue up" and wait to take turns expressing their ideas. There is a complex set of mental behaviors that occur when people think of an idea and then begin to verbally express it. The delay between idea generation and articulation interferes with the generation of the next idea. Long or unpredictable delays are particularly detrimental for teams. In one telling investigation, people working at computer terminals were assigned a creative task, but their ability to produce ideas was blocked by a computer program that simulated production blocking. The program prevented some participants from entering brainstorming ideas for a fixed period of time. This delay interfered with idea generation in two ways: (1) it disrupted the organization of idea generation when delays were relatively long; and (2) it reduced the flexibility of idea generation when delays were unpredictable.

Miss Manners Is Not a Good Brainstormer

People in groups usually try to act in a way that is acceptable to others. Being nice and agreeable, making small talk, and listening is part of what is known as the *politeness ritual*. People who are not good at it are often labeled as lacking in social skills or simply awkward. Groups usually follow a self-imposed politeness ritual that includes taking turns, which, as we have already seen, is bad for ideation. Taking turns interferes with creative idea generation at two stages of the idea-generation process: *knowledge activation* (i.e., thinking of ideas) and *idea production* (speaking up about ideas).

If one person is talking, others must remain silent, and their ideas may be forgotten by the time their turn to communicate eventually arrives. In addition, when the speaker's ideas are different from what the listener is thinking, this may have an inhibitory effect on the listener's ideas.

So, being in a group is a little like multitasking. Research clearly indicates that most people are abysmal in this regard. People who are regularly bombarded with several streams of communication often do not pay attention, or they pay attention to irrelevant things. In one investigation, researchers compared people who did a lot of media multitasking and those who did not. The groups were shown sets of two red rectangles alone or surrounded by two, four, or six blue rectangles. Each configuration was flashed twice, and participants had to determine whether the two red rectangles in the second frame were in a different position than in the first frame. Even though they were told to ignore the blue rectangles, the high-achieving multitaskers were constantly distracted by the irrelevant blue images, and they performed very badly. Moreover, it was not even the case that the self-reported high-achieving multitaskers had better memories. In all tests, they performed worse than low-achieving multitaskers because they were not able to filter out the irrelevant information from the relevant information.

Breaking the Pattern

CYBERSTORMING. What's one solution to production blocking? *Cyberstorming*. Cyberstorming is brainstorming via computers, or any other device that allows people to type into a shared database when and where they want to. Cyberstorming works because members don't have to fight for a conversational turn in a meeting; instead, they simply have to type their comments and ideas, which are immediately projected onto a screen for all to see. No production is blocked! A form of cyberstorming is becoming more popular in the classroom as well. The Sloan Consortium, an organization that tracks emerging trends and data for online education found that, in 2011, 31 percent of higher education students took at least one online course compared to students in 2008 when only 24 percent took online courses. There has been a 10 percent growth rate for online enrollments compared to only 2 percent for traditional instruction. More students asked questions via Twitter to their university instructor than through the traditional method of raising their hands. By not feeling that their questions or comments would be blocked by other students, students participated more, and learned more in the classroom. We discuss cyberstorming more in chapter 6.

BRAINWRITING. *Brainwriting* is another technique developed precisely to counter the production-blocking problem. In brainwriting, instead of team members vocalizing their ideas in an unconstrained free-for-all, team members simultaneously, but independently, write down their ideas. When each member of a team is given permission to write ideas down simultaneously amid silence in the group, the focus of attention is just on ideas—no eye contact, no turn-taking, and no politeness necessary! We'll explore brainwriting in more depth in chapter 6.

OTHER TECHNIQUES. Other solutions require a bit more work on the part of the group facilitator. I know of a group that uses a timer and when a group member has "timed out," he or she can't talk any more. I have worked with a company that gives everyone a stack of eight to ten "speaking cards" and once people play their cards, they need to be quiet. Speaking cards help ensure equal input—if team members simply take turns, there is no limit to how many turns an overly loquacious team member may take and monopolize the group.

Dumbing Down

Most people are so self-preoccupied that they falsely believe that others are constantly thinking about them. In my research with Dr. Tanya Menon of The Ohio State Business School, we discovered that most people believe that their personal assets are a threat to others when in fact others are not envious of them. We call this the "don't hate me because I'm beautiful effect." The problem is this self-serving assumption is just plain off-base—the people who we think are envious of us simply don't like us!

OK—so we are self-absorbed, preoccupied with how others view us, and wrong about how much of a threat we pose to others. What does that have to do with the creative generation of ideas? The first rule of Osborn's cardinal four rules of brainstorming is "expressiveness." Brainstorming and idea generation cannot work when people feel that they cannot express themselves. There has been a lot in this chapter about how people conform in groups and about several other negative group dynamics that conspire to squelch creativity. Another factor that can thwart the effectiveness of brainstorming groups is *evaluation apprehension*—the concern that people have that others are judging them and may feel that their ideas are silly. Whereas it is normal to be concerned about how we are viewed in the eyes of others, there are factors that can make this concern worse, or even immobilize people. As the group grows larger, concerns about evaluation apprehension increase. To the extent that a person values and admires his or her team, that person's concerns with evaluation apprehension are greater. The problem is that people who are concerned about what others think of them are more likely to behave not only in socially acceptable ways, but in ways that avoid the possibility of unfavorable evaluations—not a recipe for creative thought!

How Thin Is Your Skin?

Some people are more concerned with how they are perceived than others. Are you one of these people? The *fear of negative evaluation scale* (FNE) measures the degree with which people are concerned about being evaluated negatively. Here are a few items from the FNE.

1. I worry about what other people will think of me, even when I know it doesn't make any difference.

2. I am usually worried about what kind of impression I make.

3. I often worry that I will do or say the wrong things.

4. If I know someone is judging me, it has little effect on me.

5. Other people's opinions do not bother me.

6. I rarely worry about what kind of impression I am making on someone.

If you agreed with the first three statements, but not the last three, you are most likely high in terms of fear of negative evaluation. If you agreed with the last three statements, but not the first three, then you are extremely low in terms of fear of negative evaluation. Another way of looking at your responses is to rate yourself from 1 to 5 on each statement (1 = not characteristic of me; 5 = extremely characteristic of me). Then flip your scores on the last three items (i.e., if you gave yourself a 5 on statement 4, then convert it to a 1, and so on). An average score, according to psychologist Mark Leary, is about a 3 (indicating "moderately characteristic").

Chapter Capstone

This chapter reviewed the several factors that conspire to hinder the performance of creative teams. Taken as a whole, these factors pose some rather daunting challenges for the survival, much less success, of such teams. I am not suggesting for one minute that we eliminate teams in organizations—we do not want to disassemble teams! Rather, we want to do three things. First, we want to capitalize on what teams are good at. Teams are great at convergent thinking and good at mobilizing people within the organization. Second, we want to capitalize on what individuals are good at. Individuals working independently and not in the presence of others are good at divergent thinking. Third, we need to introduce some cost-effective best practices to aid the creative team, such as brainwriting and cyberstorming. In the chapters that follow, I introduce even more best practices that are highly cost-effective.

CHAPTER 3

Picking the Right People for the Creative Team

Like many professors, I assign group projects in my classroom. For several years, I labored under the assumption that giving students free rein to choose their teammates would result in better teamwork, if for no other reason than the exercise of freedom of choice. However, most of the time, the student projects were not stellar. And most of the teams were not particularly happy with each other by the end of the term. One year, I decided to do a turn-the-tables experiment, and announced that I was assigning the teams. I did not do it randomly, though. Rather, I dug into students' biographical information, examined where they had worked, discovered their undergraduate majors, and composed teams that were quite diverse not only in ethnicity, but in work background and training. I then waited for the complaints and secretly dreaded reading their projects. However, an astounding thing happened: the students worked harder and learned more and the projects were much more incisive. Students told me offline that they liked the team composition because they were not under pressure to be nice to their friends.

Much of the time, we don't have the luxury of selecting our teammates and collaboration partners. Rather, we work with whom we are given. If you do have the luxury of handpicking your team, think carefully about whom to put on the team, because otherwise, you may regret some of your choices.

The most fundamental decision leaders make is deciding who should be on a team. What types of skills should they have? What kind of personality is ideal? How do personalities blend on a team? For that matter, how big should the team be? How diverse should the team be? What kinds of expertise are needed? Do we need subject-matter gurus or do we need great relationship managers? The more diversity we have on the team, the more likely it is that we will have conflict. So, how should we deal with conflict?

If you don't have a headache already just thinking about those questions, you will certainly go nuts if you try to make sense of the mass of different personality tests, measures, and profiles that have been created. There is no "gold standard" when it comes to personality tests. However, there is some good news. Bottom line: there are a few key questions you need to think through and make decisions about to build your team.

Warning: some of these practices do not conform to standards of contemporary political correctness, so I apologize in advance. Some are downright nonintuitive. And get ready to take some quizzes and self-assessments.

I encourage the team leader to spend time setting the stage for the team to work creatively. It is important for the leader to avoid things like making the team too big—the most common error—and making the team too homogeneous. Once these and other potential problems have been addressed, certain personality factors can be considered. And to help you do that, this chapter introduces the science of composing creative teams on the basis of certain traits.

Don't Create a Team for the Sake of Teamwork

Above all, don't put together a team if one person can do the work. Not every project requires collaboration. Teams should be created only when there is insufficient talent on the part of any one person to achieve a clear and important goal. If one person can accomplish a task individually, then by all means, let him! Bottom line: don't force teamwork. It sours people and gives teamwork a bad name. Working together for the sake of working together does not make sense. I know of a major health-care organization that insists on a meeting to decide everything; as you might imagine, nothing ever gets done! Some organizations recognize this and appoint "benevolent dictators" to make decisions and do tasks that can be safely and competently carried out by a single person. *Collaboration should be the exception, not the norm.* When collaboration becomes the exception, then it is thoughtful and deliberate—it becomes a craft—and the conspiracy can flourish.

Keep the Team Small

Most managers assign too many people to teams and project groups. This *overstaffing bias* creates communication problems and conflict. Like the average weight of Americans, the average team is too fat—stuffed with people. Ideally, teams should be lean and mean. An investigation of scientific research teams found that the number of authors on a given publication nearly doubled from between 1955 and 2005, rising from 1.9 to 3.5 authors per paper. Similarly, James Adams and colleagues found that the size of scientific teams engaged in institutional collaboration increased 50 percent between 1981 and 1999. Gerald Marschke found that the average size of US R&D teams increased by one person (62 percent) from 1975 to 2003. I have systematically tracked the size of corporate and business teams in my research as well. My study found that the average team size prior to 2003 was 12.49. In 2009–2012, the average team size rose to 15.21; in other words, team size increased by nearly 3 people in less than a decade! By putting too many people on the team, you open a Pandora's box of unintended, negative results. Free riders are more likely to emerge as teams grow in size (chapter 2 described how increasing the size of the team is one of the best ways to encourage free riding). So don't do it! Communication problems increase exponentially as teams get larger. For example, the likelihood of scheduling a meeting for six people is infinitely more difficult than among three or four people. All the more reason to keep the number of people on a team low.

There is no firm number when it comes to right-sizing a team, but you are on the right track if you keep the following principles in mind:

- *The team editor's rule:* However big your team is now, cut it in half.

- *The single-digit rule:* Your team should never be in the double digits.

- *The bare minimum rule:* Your team should have the fewest number of people necessary to accomplish a task.

Any time that a team goes into double-digit numbers, it is in trouble. And since that's the case, our Leading High Impact Teams survey of more than one thousand team leaders indicates there *is* cause for alarm: the average number of people on a team is about thirteen people.

The most successful teams are lean in number and high in diversity—low mean and high variance. Of course, this setup comes at a cost: heterogeneity among people is a breeding ground for conflict. However, healthy debate and conflict are a good thing for teams, so handled right, this consequence actually boosts a team's creativity.

Noah Had It Wrong: We Don't Need Two of Everything!

Managers have a tendency to make the team too similar in personality and in talent. This is in part because leaders try to avoid conflict by selecting people who like each other. However, it is far more important to do good work than to avoid conflict. So, put aside political correctness and go for results! A study of one R&D company showed just how important heterogeneity is: teams that included both creative and conformist members were more likely to have a radical innovation, as compared to teams that included attentive-to-detail members, which hindered innovation. Creative members enhance conflict and hinder adherence to rules; conformists reduce conflict.

Motley Crew

The team should be a "motley crew" when it comes to backgrounds, training, and thinking styles. In one study, for example, three types of teams were compared in terms of the accuracy of their decisions and the speed of their decisions. One team was composed of "locomotors"—people who were primed to get things done and emphasize speed. A second team was composed of "assessors"—people who were primed to think things through, collect a lot of data, and mull over things. Finally, a third team was a hybrid group, composed of both locomotors and assessors. The results? The locomotor team was the fastest, but the least accurate. The assessor team was the most accurate, but the slowest. Obviously, there was a trade-off: accuracy often comes at the cost of speed. But the hybrid team was both accurate and fast—it effectively capitalized on the diverse strengths of its participants. In this sense, a synergistic gain resulted from combining both tortoises (slow, thoughtful, accurate people) and hares (fast, quick, get-it-done) people.

A near-ideal combination for maximizing creativity is a team diverse in terms of background, but similar in terms of thought categories. In other words, for group diversity to be maximally effective, the distances between the kinds of ideas that members bring to the table should not be too great because people need some basis for mutual understanding of ideas. For example, in one investigation, Asako Miura and his collaborator composed groups that were either high or low on *diversity*—as defined by the range of different ideas that individual members brought to the task—and high or low in terms of *similarity*—as defined in terms of the amount of duplication of ideas they generated in an independent task. The results indicated that groups who were diverse in their *range* of ideas but similar in the *kinds* of ideas they generated were the most creative.

The Onion Principle

There are hundreds of ways to diversify. What's the best? Get to the *inside* of the onion. I often tell my students to think of diversity like an onion, meaning that there are several layers. On the outside of the onion are superficial characteristics, such as dress and appearance; the next layer is composed of characteristics such as race or ethnicity; deeper inside are education and values; and even deeper inside are fundamental personality characteristics and individual traits. It is more impactful to diversify at deeper levels. However, even superficial diversity (e.g., demographic and ethnic background) may improve creativity. One investigation compared all-white groups with groups composed of white, African American, Asian American, and Hispanic American participants. In this study, the ideas produced by ethnically diverse groups were more effective, more feasible, and of higher quality than those produced by the homogenous groups. In another study, European Americans were more creative immediately after being exposed to American and Chinese cultures, and the effect lasted for seven days. However, other investigations have not found appreciable differences. So this type of diversity may be less reliable than deeper differences in instigating creative performance.

One problem with building diverse teams is that people tend to be attracted to homogeneous groups. A compounding problem is that even when people know they should be focusing on diversity—the inside of the onion is hard to see. Ideally, we should compose teams that have deep-level diversity, but that is hard to do because sometimes those underlying skills, values, and orientations are just not obvious. What's more important than combining superficially homogeneous groups is maximizing the deep-level diversity (the inside of the onion) based on education, training, and experience. Teams with greater educational specialization heterogeneity working under transformational leaders are more creative than more homogeneous teams. In a landmark study of creativity in biotechnology laboratories in the United States and the United Kingdom, Kevin Dunbar studied teams of microbiologists and their laboratories. Some of the labs followed homogeneous hiring practices; some were heterogeneous. To be sure, the heterogeneous labs had more reported conflict, but they also produced significantly more patents!

Diversity has a number of benefits, in addition to increasing creative idea generation. For example, diversity can also provide a buffer when groups grow too large. In one study, six different numerical group sizes were studied, ranging from five to ten members. Whereas the average contributions per group member diminished with increasing group size for homogeneous groups, heterogeneous groups improved their performance.

Avoid the San Andreas Fault

According to Keith Murnighan, when some teams diversify, they create a dangerous fault line that calls negative attention to the team, which sets the team up for an earthquake. A fault line occurs in a team when there is a big divide along two or more dimensions among members. For example, suppose in a group of six people there are three men and three women. Suppose also the men are engineers and the women are human resource managers. This is an example of a fault line because two demographics— gender and functional background—divide the group. Among all the fault lines that can threaten groups, gender is one that is particularly problematic. For example, studies of teams working on creativity tasks indicate that gender fault lines negatively affect the number of ideas and overall creativity of ideas.

Avoid People Who Remind You of Yourself

There is a pervasive tendency for leaders to unconsciously choose people in their own image—part of the *egocentrism effect*. This "just like me" effect is so strong that people even tend to prefer those who have similar letters in their names; indeed people are more likely to marry a person whose name includes a high number of similar alphabet letters! *Implicit egoism* is the term for the way we are unconsciously attracted to people, things, and ideas that . . . well, remind us of our wonderful selves. But such choices lead to many problems and a boring team.

Pick Smart People

This is certainly not a politically correct piece of advice. However, the data are virtually indisputable: smart people are more creative. General cognitive ability—your IQ—predicts performance in both educational and vocational settings. Perhaps even more depressing (and even less politically correct) is the fact that it is not easy (perhaps impossible) to stimulate low-cognitive-ability people to greater creativity. For example, in one study, high- and low-cognitive ability people received either high- or low-quality stimulation (via exposure to idea submissions from group members). Not surprisingly, high-cognitive-ability people who were given high-quality stimulation performed the best; the low-cognitive-ability people were completely unaffected by good or bad stimulation. This suggests that low-cognitive-ability people are unresponsive to even the best leaders and the most stimulating environments! Bottom line: go for smarties!

That said, avoid narcissists. Narcissists are not more creative than others, but they *think* they are and they are adept at persuading others to agree with their ideas. In one investigation, narcissists rated themselves as extremely creative, but blind coders saw no differences between the creative products offered by those low or high on narcissism. So how do you know if someone is a narcissist? Narcissists are more likely to agree to the following questions: "If I ruled the world, it would be a better place" (N) versus "The thought of ruling the world frightens the hell out of me" (non-N); "I am an extraordinary person" (N) versus "I am much like everybody else" (non-N); and "I always know what I'm doing" (N) versus "Sometimes I am not sure of what I am doing" (non-N).

The SCIENCE of Personality

When it comes to personality, there are a million different tests. To make sense of all the research, I've developed an acronym to guide how we should leverage the variety of personalities on a team. This method is based on how scientific studies of personality correlate to creativity, innovation, and ideation. The acronym SCIENCE captures seven key personality dimensions that provide a reasonable guide for choosing team members:

S: *Situationists*

C: *Curiosity*

I: *Idealists*

E: *Extroverts*

N: *Non-anxious people*

C: *Low-need-for-closure people*

E: *Openness to experience*

Each is explained below. Keep in mind, this is an ideal. You may not hit all seven indicators. The advantage is that it is research-based. I will give you examples of people who are high and low on each of the dimensions described. You may even want to test yourself!

Situationists

Situationists are people who reject imposed rules and instead, advocate individual analysis of each act in each situation. They are relativists, rather than absolutists. For example, if someone used a gun to kill someone in self-defense, but lived in a city in which gun ownership was illegal, the absolutist would look primarily at the law. In contrast, the situationist would look at the extenuating factors. In this sense, situationists see possibility in every context. Conversely, absolutists or universalists tend to see black and white; they believe that the best possible outcome can always be achieved by following universal moral rules. Creative people are less likely than noncreative people to follow universal rules and truths. However, creative people are not less caring about others. In fact, creative people are high in idealism, highly caring, and have a pragmatic but moral decision-making style.

Curiosity

Curiosity may have killed the cat, but it helped the creative team. Most humans are born with an innate need to understand our world. This is *epistemic motivation*—the intense need to understand the world and how it works. For example, when someone experiences a rewarding outcome, such as getting someone to say yes to a request, they often analyze what they did and try to make it happen again. Creative people often display this thirst for understanding. People low in curiosity or epistemic motivation are largely uninterested in understanding the how and why of cause and effect in their world. Teams produce more ideas when members are high rather than low in epistemic motivation. What's more, people who are high in epistemic motivation don't appear to get defensive in the face of critical feedback. One investigation illustrates this: people received feedback from an "evaluator" (really a trained actor) via video. The feedback was either delivered in an angry way or a neutral way. The people high in epistemic motivation showed more creativity in terms of the quantity, variety, and originality of their ideas after receiving "angry" feedback, while those with low epistemic motivation were less creative. This suggests that curious people are also curious about themselves. When curious people are surprised or experience change, they seek to understand it.

People who are high in epistemic motivation are more likely to agree to statements like: "It upsets me to go into a situation without knowing what I can expect from it"; and "I enjoy having a clear and structured mode of life"; and "I find that a consistent routine enables me to enjoy life more." In contrast, people who are low in epistemic motivation are more likely to say, "I enjoy being spontaneous"; "A life well-ordered with regular hours makes life tedious"; and "I enjoy the exhilaration of being in unpredictable situations." It may seem paradoxical that curious people would prefer consistency. But this is highly consistent with the creative conspiracy principle that rules benefit the creative team process. The key is that curious people don't like it when things are unpredictable or not understood.

Idealists

The idealistic person has a genuine concern for others. Idealists display an ethic of caring and often insist that one must always avoid harming others. In fact, any creative idea or solution that may harm others will likely be unacceptable to an idealist. For this reason, it would appear that creative people would not be idealistic. Idealists are people who agree to statements such as: "One should never psychologically or physically harm another person" and "Risks to another should never be tolerated, irrespective of how small the risks might be." Paul Bierly and his colleagues measured the complex relationship between creativity and idealism. Creativity was measured by three indicators: having original ideas, solving tasks in unique ways, and being stimulating. Participants were also asked how much they agreed with statements such as "People should make certain that their actions never intentionally harm another even to a small degree." The researchers initially expected a reverse relationship between idealism and creativity; that is, the more idealistic people are, the less creative they were expected to be. The results surprised them: idealistic people were in fact *more* creative than less idealistic people! The question is, why? It may very well be that for people to work creatively, they need a supportive environment, and that caring about the welfare of others in that environment is critical for long-term success. A caring environment may promote passion about work and spur greater drive and motivation.

In another study, people were measured for openness to experience, unconventionality, ambition, and autonomy at age twenty-one and followed through their middle age. The most creative achievers in middle age were those who had been the most open, unconventional, ambitious, and autonomous at age twenty-one. What was particularly noteworthy was that the most creative people in middle age had made a behavioral commitment early in life.

Extroverts

Extroverts are people who seek out the presence of others. There is decent evidence that extroverts make good team members. Teams composed primarily of people with personality characteristics conducive to team creativity (high extroversion, high openness to experience, and low conscientiousness) show synergistic increases in creativity when their team confidence level is high. Most people know if they are introverts or extroverts, but sometimes it is hard to guess what others are. Extroverts are more likely to agree with the following: "I am: talkative, full of energy, assertive in personality, outgoing, and sociable." In contrast, introverts are more likely to agree with the following: "I am: reserved, quiet, shy, and inhibited."

Non-Anxious People

People who are highly socially anxious are inhibited. They self-censor and fall into uncomfortable silence around others. Not surprisingly, people high in dispositional anxiousness are less creative than people low in dispositional anxiousness. Moreover, when non-anxious people are in the presence of anxious people, they start to feel anxious! Simply stated, non-anxious individuals lower their performance on creative tasks in the direction of highly anxious people. As with extroverts, most people probably know if they themselves are the anxious type, but anxiety is sometimes hard to quickly discern in others. What are the key giveaways? Anxious people feel nervous and tense when they are in social situations, job interviews, parties, on the phone, speaking with leaders, and talking with people who are different from themselves. Strangers, people of the opposite sex, authority figures, and audiences generally bring out anxiety. One way of overcoming anxiety is to create trust within the team.

Low-Need-for-Closure People

The high-need-for-closure person likes to reach conclusions and resolve matters quickly and neatly. In contrast, the low-need-for-closure person can live with (and even thrive on) ambiguity, uncertainty, and lack of clarity. In one study, teams attempted to create advertising slogans for a product. Some of the teams were composed of people low in need for closure; others were high in need for closure. The low-need-for-closure teams showed more ideational fluency, elaboration of ideas, and creativity as rated by independent judges. Unlike anxiety and extraversion, need for closure is something that people often don't have as much self-awareness about. Consider the following pairs of phrases: "Having clear rules and order at work is essential for success" versus "Even after I have made up my mind about something, I am always eager to consider a different opinion"; "I do not usually consult many different opinions before forming my own view" versus "I prefer interacting with people whose opinions are very different from my own"; "I'd rather know bad news than stay in a state of uncertainty" versus "I tend to put off making important decisions until the last possible moment"; and "I'd like to know what people are thinking about most of the time" versus "When considering a conflict, I can usually see how both sides could be right." If you tended to resonate with the first statement in each pair, you have a high need for closure. If you resonated with the second statement in each pair, you are lower in need for closure.

Openness to Experience

Openness to experience is a personality construct that includes willingness to try new things, be uncomfortable, and step away from routine. This type of mind-set focuses on big-picture thinking rather than narrow thinking. This is the mind-set that looks at the forest rather than focusing on a single tree. In a provocative study of employees from a large global firm, those who scored high on openness as well as had networks characterized by high diversity, were the most creative. Moreover, teams whose members have different levels of openness to experience have the highest levels of team creativity, as long as they have some team members who are low on openness and others who have a moderate level of openness to experience. What are the telltale signs that people are high in openness to experience? They are more likely to vote for liberal political candidates, say that they believe in the importance of art, listen to new ideas, have a vivid imagination, and in general carry conversations to a higher level. People who are low in openness to experience are more likely to vote for conservative political candidates, have no liking for art or art museums, and avoid philosophical discussions and abstract ideas. Groups that have open-mindedness norms as well as a norm of decision comprehensiveness are more likely to have open, rigorous discussions.

Chapter Capstone

When staffing the creative team, choose the fewest number of people possible (if that means just you, then fine—there is no point in collaborating for collaboration's sake). Alternatively, fire yourself from the team and set an example. Choose people who are different from you in style and talent. Don't be afraid to choose people you don't like. It is more important to *respect* your teammates than to *like* them. Be nonpolitical (don't put people on the team for any reason other than the fact that they have the talent necessary to accomplish the goal). If you want to focus on personality, then go for the SCIENCE traits—situationism, curiosity, idealism, extroversion, non-anxiety, low need for closure, and openness to experience.

CHAPTER 4

Leading the Creative Team

Recently, a newly appointed senior manager from a major company attended my course. On the first day, Sheila offered to the class that she had been tapped to lead a highly diverse, extremely decentralized team in her organization. Sheila admitted that this would be her first leadership challenge at such a level. This would be a new role for her. Sheila's biggest fear was that the team would not accept her as a leader. When I asked her why, she explained that several more senior "insiders" had not been promoted to lead the team, and she had been brought in from a different group. Many of the people who used to be Sheila's peers were now her direct reports. Sheila felt resentment in the air. In short, she was petrified. She needed an action plan.

This chapter provides an action plan for leading the creative team. It is composed of several conversations that leaders need to have with their teams. Too often, we see leaders who have an urgent need to sit down and get to the business at hand. Meanwhile, the eight-hundred-pound gorilla in the room is the unspoken conversations that should be occurring between the leader and the team, namely: What is our goal? What do we expect from the leader? What do we expect from one another? What do I do if this is not working for me?

Pseudo Goals and Authentic Goals

Goals are the defining characteristics of teams. A group is a collection of people; a team is a group of people with a shared objective. A creative team works with the conviction that collectively they can achieve more than they could working independently—that is, they deeply believe the whole is greater than the sum of the parts. In our work with teams, my colleagues and I often spend quite a bit of time on goals. In one top management team meeting I facilitated, I suspected that the group did not share a clearly defined goal, so I passed out index cards and instructed everyone to write a one-sentence statement about what they thought *others* wanted as the goal and then, on a separate card, what the goal *should be*. I collected the cards, shuffled them, and distributed them randomly among the members. We then read them aloud, but preserved anonymity: no one was allowed to guess who said what, and no one was allowed to say, "I said that." The point was to have a conversation about the goals of the group that was independent of the people who authored the cards.

The entire group then worked to sort cards into piles with similar themes. We first took on the task of what people *thought* the goal was. We called this the *pseudo goal*. Pseudo goals are not actually what anybody wants, but rather what we *think* others want. As suspected, the responses were not only all over the map, but several were completely contradictory. We found almost no agreement. And there was not a great deal of passion.

We then shuffled and distributed the set of cards that represented what people really wanted the goal to be and did the same thing. We called this the *authentic goal*. We quickly noticed two things: there was slightly more agreement about the goal, and there was most definitely more passion and clarity.

We spent the rest of our time drawing up a team charter using the authentic goal cards. We went through several iterations of sorting cards, and eventually, the group converged on a clear and compelling mission statement. The team agreed to revisit the mission statement within the next four months.

Excavating Expectations

Once the team has a clear goal, it is imperative to lay out the day-to-day working expectations. Some groups set lofty and compelling goals, only to disappoint one another because they failed to understand their working expectations. This is because our expectations are often unspoken. They remain below the surface of a group's conscious awareness and are usually not part of the team conversation. The key is to surface expectations early on so the group has an idea of what is expected of them. This is the process of *excavating expectations*.

Must-Haves, Would-Likes, and No-No's

The sky's the limit when it comes to laying out expectations. I usually begin the excavation by asking each person to write five must-haves, five would-likes, and five no-no's. With regard to the "must-haves," all members of the team are asked to specify what they feel they *cannot live without*. It is important to note that this is not the time to make a list of resources that the group would *like* to have. Anything that is written down on these cards must be something that the people in the room have the power to either contribute or deny to others. This rules out asking for a new IT system, an increased operating budget, or requesting that so-and-so should be fired. For example, one team generated the following as "must-haves": start meetings on time, be prepared, and give 24-hour notice if you can't attend a meeting.

Most people have strong notions of what they expect and want from others. However, these wants and needs are often unspoken. *Psychological contracts* are the unspoken rules of engagement that people expect others to share. They develop unconsciously over time. Nevertheless, they are powerful. Once expectations are violated by an unwitting team member, a breach occurs, and then resentment brews.

I usually ask team members to also list behaviors and actions that they would *like to have* in a group—but that they consider luxuries—meaning that they are not essential but nevertheless are valued. By surfacing the "would-likes," team members get a sense of what to expect from one another. One group that I worked with came up with the following "would-likes": meetings should be no longer than sixty to ninety minutes and should have a check-in for five minutes at the beginning of the meeting—as opposed to immediately getting down to work.

The list of no-no's are important for teams to discuss before a violation has occurred. Anything is fair game here. One group that I worked with had four no-no's that they considered mission critical to avoid in their team meetings: checking e-mail and cell phone messages, taking cell phone calls, making cell phone calls, and interrupting others.

Get on the Tightrope

Once a goal is clarified and expectations are outlined, the team needs to get on with the work at hand. Unfortunately, leaders often fail to get out of the way of their team. I call this *being on the tightrope* because it is a balancing act: The key is not to disappear, but also not to intrude.

Let's return to Sheila. At one extreme, she could dictate the team's goal, bark out orders, and command the team to perform. At the other extreme, she could sit behind the stage and simply watch her team try to perform. Obviously, these are ridiculous extremes, and Sheila needed to be somewhere in between. I shared with her four ideas based on Richard Hackman's *The Design of Work Teams* and asked her to envision which style she thought would work best with the team.

> *Top-down leadership*: This style would give Sheila the most control. In such a model, she would have the ultimate say in selecting the team, determining its size, setting goals, outlining performance expectations, monitoring the team's success, and evaluating team results. Top-down leadership is a good team design choice when team members

are naive, have little experience, and need a lot of direction, and when the leader has the time and energy to invest. They might also be a good choice in hierarchical organizations, where reporting relationships are clearly outlined.

Self-managing team: A better design choice for Sheila's team might be a *self-managing team.* Self-managing teams set their own performance expectations and goals, and monitor their own progress. Leaders are there to support and guide the team when needed. In this case, Sheila would collaborate with the team on a goal, but leave it to the team to decide on how to reach the goal.

Self-designing team: Another design option for Sheila is the *self-directing* or *self-designing team.* Self-designing teams make most of the decisions, plot their own course, select and recruit their own members, and consult the leader as needed. In this case, Sheila would relinquish control of the team's recruitment of new members to the team itself. This may be a good idea if the team is aware of the talents of other members in the organization and they have effective networks.

Self-governing team: A self-governing team does all the things that a self-designing team does, but also has a much broader range of influence and authority over the larger organization.

Overmanaged or Underled?

To make an informed team design choice, Sheila needs to consider the experience and knowledge level of the team members, as well as her own knowledge and expertise. In addition, Sheila needs to consider the norms of the larger organization. I emphasized to Sheila that team design should be a conscious decision. In practical terms, Sheila needs to think through just what she wants to control and decide how much autonomy she wants to give the team. It is imperative to be transparent about expectations with her team before they begin their work. If Sheila does not have this open conversation about expectations, the risk she takes is that people will feel either overmanaged or underled. In other words, if Sheila is treating the team in a top-down fashion, but members believe they are capable of self-direction, she will be viewed as overmanaging or micromanaging the team. Similarly, if Sheila is taking a background role but the team members need her guidance, she will be viewed as an absent leader.

In my research, that tracks leaders' self-assessments of their own styles, I discovered that the dominant team leadership style is a self-managing team—52 percent of team leaders describe their own style this way. The second-most-popular style is manager-led—42 percent of leaders report using that style; and only about 6 percent use a self-directing style. However, when I take a deeper look at those leaders who primarily lead creative teams, it is twice as likely that these leaders use a self-directing style (12 percent), suggesting that leaders of creative teams are more likely to empower their team than those leading problem-solving and tactical teams.

Plan on Change

The chances that a leader is going to perfectly hit the mark with his or her team is slim to none. So I tell leaders to plan on not being perfect, to stop moping and blaming others, and to instead get feedback and figure out what they need to do differently.

Too often leaders treat their teams purely as a task or a job and are not open to changing their style or approach midcourse. Whether leaders realize it or not, leading a team means being in a relationship. Excellent leaders talk about their relationship with their team, how they want to improve it, and what they would like to work on. A large-scale, longitudinal investigation of 828 employees on 116 teams working in a Chinese iron and steel manufacturing company tested this hypothesis. Over a six-month period, supervisors displayed high levels of respect for and trust in their employees to see if this affected the employees' self-efficiency and creativity. The relationship the leaders had with their team members revealed that employees' self-efficacy—the belief that they could accomplish something—rose from 72 percent satisfaction to 82 percent, and also had a positive effect on creativity.

What might Sheila do with regard to building the relationship? Consider three key objectives: (1) communicate her leadership style, (2) ask for feedback from her team, and (3) discuss how each group member could either sabotage the team or work to make it a success. The last question was a potential can of worms, but Sheila was encouraged to be open and candid about how each member of the team had the power to either help or dismantle the team. It was also probable that if Sheila asked for the team's support, they would be less likely to work against her.

Once Sheila has done all the above, her work does not end. Every leader is a work in progress. Thus, Sheila needs to think about how she might seek feedback on a regular basis from the team as to her effectiveness. I proposed two formats: (1) one-on-one and (2) team-based. First, Sheila can meet with her team members on a one-on-one basis periodically. I cautioned Sheila to *not* ask, "How am I doing?" This is an evaluative question that puts pressure on the respondent to simply say, "Fine" or "OK" or perhaps, "Awful." If you want to learn and grow, avoid asking questions that can be answered with a single word. Rather, I encouraged Sheila to ask, "What would you like to see more of from me? Less of from me?" In other words, excellent collaborative leaders formulate questions that give permission to the other person to give feedback. For team-based feedback, I encouraged Sheila to periodically ask the group three questions: (1) What's working for this group? (2) What needs changing? and (3) What is missing that should be added?

Not only will you learn from every experience if you change your line of questioning, your boss apparently will take notice, too! People who ask for feedback are rated by their supervisors as more creative. What's more, those who solicit feedback directly and monitor the environment for indirect feedback achieve more creative outcomes.

However Much Feedback You Think People Need, Double It

Most people are starved for feedback, and most of all, they want feedback from their leaders. In fact, the Millennials who have now joined the business world like to know how they're doing weekly or even daily. Millennials were raised with so much affirmation and positive reinforcement that they come into the workplace expecting such discussion. This is a generation treated so delicately that many schoolteachers stopped grading papers and tests in red ink. Managers have reported cases of Millennials breaking down in tears after a negative performance review, some going so far as to quit their jobs. In MBA programs, instructors receive grade inquiries from the parents of twenty-six-year-old students.

To be sure, a big part of teamwork is to grow and develop team members. For this reason it is imperative to give members the right type of feedback. Consider the distinction between informational feedback and evaluative feedback. *Informational evaluations* don't apply pressure but instead give useful information. An example is, "Anyone can solve problems by coming up with conventional solutions, but the employee who is creative and offers unique ideas stands out. This evaluation will help you learn something that will be useful to you in the future. Remember, we are interested in your creativity." *Controlling evaluations*, in contrast, use features that achieve a specific outcome, or pressure to perform. For example, "You are going to be judged on how creative you are by experts in human resources, who are knowledgeable and tough. These experts will critically evaluate your solutions to the problems by analyzing every point you make in the memo and judging if it is creative or not." In a study that compared the impact of both types of evaluations, people were more creative and more intrinsically motivated when they anticipated an *informational* evaluation rather than a *controlling* evaluation.

Be Honest: Does This Sound Like You?

What are the characteristics of leaders who have particularly successful teams? Excellent leaders exhibit these eight key behaviors and characteristics.

1. EXCELLENT LEADERS HAVE A LANGUAGE THAT ALLOWS THEM TO TALK ABOUT THEIR LEADERSHIP STYLE. Excellent leaders consciously and explicitly communicate their style to others; they explain themselves and the rationale for using their approach. Sheila was encouraged to self-describe her intended leadership style in behavioral terms and talk about the relationship between herself and the team.

2. EXCELLENT LEADERS ENGAGE IN RECIPROCAL COMMUNICATION. Excellent leaders ask questions like, "What aspects of my style are working for you?"; "What aspects are not working?"; "What should I do more of?"; "Less of?" Excellent leaders assume there are aspects of their leadership style that are not working for everyone and take steps to identify them.

3. EXCELLENT LEADERS ARE ON A PERSONAL DEVELOPMENT MISSION. Excellent leaders involve their team in their own personal development mission ("I could be better; this is what I'm working on now," etc.) and they simultaneously support their team as they grow and learn. I warned Sheila that just like other leaders, she will probably disappoint, or even frustrate her team and when this happens, instead of sulking or blaming others, she should seek feedback.

4. EXCELLENT LEADERS OFFER DEVELOPMENTAL FEEDBACK. Excellent leaders do not shy away or avoid conversations that focus on how people can improve. Whereas it is often more comfortable to simply praise others, really good leaders approach every interaction as a chance for personal improvement—in themselves and others. Most people want much more feedback from their leaders than they actually get. I coached Sheila to plan on giving about double the amount of feedback she believes people need from her.

5. EXCELLENT LEADERS DISPLAY INTERACTIONAL JUSTICE. People want to be treated fairly. For example, a study of creativity among dissatisfied employees reveals that even when job dissatisfaction is high, employees will be creative if they get useful feedback from coworkers and feel that their organization is supporting them. This is why it is imperative that Sheila have a well-thought-out leadership style that she can consistently and accurately describe to others.

6. EXCELLENT LEADERS ARE TRUSTWORTHY. Excellent leaders earn trust through behavioral consistency and by focusing on the higher goals of the organization. Leaders put personal self-interest aside and focus on the mission.

7. EXCELLENT LEADERS HAVE AN AMBIDEXTROUS STYLE. Excellent leaders have the ability to switch seamlessly between exploring and exploiting behavior for the purposes of ideation and production. Exploration is the creative aspect—the relentless motivation to keep trying new things and experimenting, even if that means making mistakes. In contrast, exploitation is the get-it-right-and-then-stick-with-it aspect—the need to develop airtight procedures that will guarantee consistent results. These two activities are complementary in the sense that one is an opening-up approach (exploration) and the other is closing (getting to market). The key point is that to be an effective creative collaborative leader, the hybrid model—one that uses both approaches—is necessary. As an example, consider a team that perfects a certain product. They rigorously test it and then eliminate all errors and it works flawlessly. However, time passes, and new companies enter the market and new technologies develop that begin to date the product. The team needs to experiment with how to refine the product in light of the changing environment.

3M would never have developed the smashingly successful Post-it Notes if the glue had actually worked as intended. In 1968, 3M chemist Spencer Silver developed a high-quality but "low-tack" adhesive made of tiny, indestructible acrylic spheres that would stick only where they were tangent to a given surface. Over a period of five years, Silver shared his product idea with colleagues at 3M, informally and in seminar presentations. A marketable use of the product proved elusive, and Silver's temporary adhesive was deemed useless by the company—until colleague Art Fry attended one of Silver's company presentations and had a brainstorm. Fry, an employee of 3M's New Product Development lab, had been frustrated by the fact that, in church, when he opened his hymnal, the paper bookmarks that he used to mark the songs on the program would slip out. Fry, daydreaming during a dull sermon, realized that Silver's reusable adhesive would solve this problem. Returning to work, Fry wrote up his idea for a reliable, reusable bookmark and presented it to his supervisors. Management worried that the product would seem wasteful and nearly scrapped the idea. But minds were changed when the 3M office staff loved the initial samples. It took another five years to perfect the specifications and design machines to manufacture the notes, but in 1980, Post-it Notes were introduced nationwide.

The ambidextrous leader switches between exploring and exploiting styles to deal with the evolving requirements of the innovation process. In short, the team needs permission to experiment and fail in order to eventually succeed.

8. EXCELLENT LEADERS ARE TRANSFORMATIONAL. *Transactional leaders* treat leadership like a bank account. They make investments in people and expect returns; they keep track of costs and expenses, they measure things like productivity, efficiency, cost, and so on, and they approach relationships as a series of discrete transactions. They use carrots and sticks. This style of leadership assumes that people are inherently extrinsically motivated by seeking rewards and avoiding punishments. Transactional leaders tend to endorse these kinds of leadership beliefs: "I discuss in specific terms who is responsible for achieving performance targets"; "I provide others with assistance in exchange for their efforts"; "I discuss in specific terms who is responsible for achieving performance

targets"; "I display a sense of power and confidence"; and "I keep track of all mistakes."

In contrast, *transformational* leaders focus on goals as a unifying, igniting device. They don't see individual transactions; they see possibilities and a web of relationships. Transformational leaders tend to resonate more with these types of beliefs: "I talk about my most important values and beliefs"; "I talk enthusiastically about what needs to be accomplished"; "I specify the importance of having a strong sense of purpose"; "I articulate a compelling vision of the future"; and "I help others develop their strengths."

Transactional leaders hold a strong belief that work needs to be specific, performance expectations need to be clear, and rewards need to be forthcoming if the job is accomplished or punished if the job is not done. Conversely, transformational leaders don't rely on the carrot-and-stick approach to motivate people, rather, they set a vision and set their team free, showing confidence in their ability to accomplish the vision.

Transformational leaders are more likely to engender creative employees. They influence employee creativity through psychological empowerment. The positive relationship between transformational leadership and team creativity is even stronger when the leader is strong in task and relational support. Similar positive results for transformational leadership have been observed in developing countries and newly developed industries. Transformational leadership also is related to increased creativity in collectivist cultures, such as South Korea's.

Traps to Avoid

People hold high expectations of leaders, and leaders who make missteps are evaluated harshly. Below, I outline potential leadership traps: the power trap, the knowledge trap, and the confirmation trap.

The Power Trap

The *power trap* is the insidious tendency for those in power to potentially be consumed by it. For example, people who have power behave in ways that are riskier and more insensitive than those who are not in power. On the one hand, powerful people are not afraid of playing devil's advocate, but they can often be insensitive to those around them. Powerful people generate more creative ideas, conform less to others' opinions, and are more influenced by their own value system. But they are also more likely to interrupt others, make risky decisions, and outright ignore others. And the effects of power on human behavior can be triggered by quite subtle cues, such as seating arrangements and arbitrary designations.

I asked Sheila about how she uses power. Specifically, I asked her to think about something she wanted to achieve in the past month that required an influence attempt on her part. Some of the things she listed included: trying to get a client to agree to change a deliverable date; asking colleagues for more resources; trying to gain inclusion into an important project or group or presentation; trying to change job responsibilities or perks; and trying to change the time of a meeting. I then asked her to think about what she did to influence the team. People use power in different ways to get what they want. Most of the time, we are not consciously aware of how we are using power. The five most common sources of power are:

> *Legitimate*: Legitimate power is based on a person's formal position. The target of legitimate power complies because of a belief in the legitimacy of the power holder. I know of a professor who insists that all subordinates—students, staff, and so on—call him by his formal title. I also know of some company leaders who are quick to find out the status and title of others in their organization and how many direct reports they have. In our example, Sheila might

simply announce to her group that she holds the job title that requires that her subordinates comply with her. Leaders who are low in organizational status are more effective when they use a directive style, so as to establish their authority. Conversely, leaders who enjoy high organizational status are viewed as more effective when they use a participative style.

Reward: Reward power is based on a person's ability to grant rewards; the other person complies because of a desire to receive rewards. For example, Sheila might promise certain benefits or rewards to her team if they work with her.

Coercive: Coercive power is based on a person's ability to punish. The other person complies because of a fear of punishment. For example, Shelia might threaten members of her team with a poor performance review or unattractive assignments if they fail to comply.

Expert: Expert power is based on personal expertise in a certain area. The target of influence complies because of a belief in the power holder's knowledge. For example, an expert witness holds a lot of power and influence in a jury trial because of their depth of knowledge of a subject. In many ways, expertise and experience is what Shelia fears she is most lacking. She fears that the members of her team do not see her as skilled enough to lead the team.

Referent: Sometimes, a person's power is based on the fact that they are respected, attractive, trustworthy, and nice. The classic Vicks Formula 44 cough syrup television commercial in which two spokesmen successively pitched the over-the-counter medication with the line, "I'm not a doctor, but I play one on TV" relied on referent power. The spokesmen were soap opera actors Chris Robinson (who played Dr. Rick Webber on *General Hospital*) and Peter Bergman (who played Dr. Cliff Warner on *All My Children*). The actors were quick to admit they did not have legitimate nor expert power but were instead relying on the fact that people liked the characters they played. Referent power is based on a person's attractiveness to others. The target audience complies because they respect and like the power holder. Often this is the type of power that highly charismatic and attractive people use. It is unclear whether Sheila possesses such power. And even if she does, she does not feel confident in her ability to pull her team together.

Bottom line: leaders who use legitimate, referent, and expert power are evaluated more favorably than those who use coercive power and even reward power. Leaders who let power go to their heads are in trouble because they often become more verbally dominant—in short, they talk too much! When leaders are verbally dominant, the team sees them as less open to ideas and communication. For this reason, I cautioned Sheila to let others talk and minimize her own pontifications.

The Knowledge Trap

The *knowledge trap* is the faulty belief held by leaders that they must know more than others and have the ultimate answer. This ego-driven perspective may imperil the ability of subordinates to suggest new ideas. It is not surprising, then, that some teams work around the leader or the larger organization. They may meet at night or even have separate e-mail accounts and code names if they suspect that the larger organization is not supportive. *Creative deviance* refers to such actions taken by employees who choose to buck their leader's orders and pursue new ideas ex officio/on their own authority. The Pontiac Fiero, the first midsized commercial car in the United States, was developed after orders from upper management to stop working on the project were ignored. The film *The Godfather* was born when a filmmaker disregarded Paramount Pictures' orders about where the story should take place, the budget, and the cast.

The Nordstrom Innovation Lab is an example of leadership that knows how to avoid the knowledge trap. It's an edgy start-up inside of Nordstrom that meets every week after hours to figure out how to do things better the next week. The team builds a new product every week and fully expects 30 percent to fail completely. If these employees did not experiment with creative deviance and if they believed that upper management had all the answers—then the culture-changing products that they create would never be born. Teams are more likely to experiment with creative deviance when the organization places a relatively greater value on creativity than conformity. What's the catch? By inviting creativity, organizations create uncertainty because no one can predict whether the pursuit of a new idea will actually result in a positive outcome.

The Confirmation Trap

The *confirmation trap* is the tendency for leaders to say that they want others to speak their minds, when in fact they really want others to agree with them. In short, leaders want others to give the appearance of being thoughtful and comfortable with controversy, but in the end, they want others to confirm their own ideas. Winston Churchill was intimately aware of the powerful confirmation trap and how it could place a stranglehold on effective leadership. For that reason, when he developed the Central Statistical Office in World War II, he expressly told his team to "bring me the bleakest, most depressing news." Churchill recognized the negative effects of the confirmation trap. When teams believe that leaders want to hear only certain messages or good news, this blocks the flow of essential information and can threaten creative collaboration. *Groupthink* is often a consequence of the confirmation trap in which team members self-censor their own doubts and rationalize inconsistent information so as to agree with what they believe the team—and the leader—wants to hear. The creative collaboration approach stands in sharp contrast to the dysfunctional groupthink process. However, the creative collaboration process must be deliberately engineered—just like Churchill did with the Central Statistical Office—the leader of the creative team must set the stage for bad news and controversy to be expressed.

◄ Chapter Capstone

As a leader, you've got a lot on your shoulders. It begins with articulating the mission. Too often, teams begin without having a mission or a map. Once the leader has clearly articulated the mission, it is imperative to excavate the working expectations. Too often, these are unspoken and team members innocently violate one another's assumptions. Leaders need to strike a delicate balance between letting the team do its work and overseeing the team. The leader who gives the team a preview of how he or she leads has a much better chance of meeting a team's expectations. The likelihood that leaders will perfectly hit the elusive mark of being the person that the team has envisioned as their leader is a long shot. So leaders should anticipate that they will disappoint their team and then figure out how to quickly get data on what they should do differently.

CHAPTER 5

Motivating the Creative Team

One graduate student (let's call him Tim) at the university had near-perfect standardized test scores and a magna cum laude grade point average. Another student (George) barely squeaked into the program with mediocre test scores and an unimpressive GPA. In fact, if it had not been for a sudden movement on the waiting list, George would not have been admitted to the program. As I watched these two students over the next twelve months, I witnessed a curious development in their success as young scholars. Tim, the "brilliant" student with all the raw talent had a hard time choosing a thesis topic, started and then abandoned several research projects, and turned down several opportunities for research and writing projects that others would have leaped at. In contrast, George, the "mediocre" student, constantly asked questions, badgered me to read his latest research proposal, and took on several projects that required him to work weekends and evenings in the laboratory and at his computer. When I asked him if he was stressed, however, his eyes lit up and he went on to tell me that he was going to run another lab study that week. At the end of the year, Tim took an unspecified "leave of absence"; in contrast, George had his paper accepted by the most prestigious professional society of his discipline. A decade later, no one has ever cared to ask either of these people what their standardized scores were.

In my experience as a professor, I have witnessed no less than eight times a student with perfect test scores unable to make it through grad school. I have also witnessed some students who don't have perfect scores evolve into talented, energetic, and successful scholars. The relentless hunger that prompts one person to stay up all night trying to solve an enigma, craft an interesting research question, or redesign an experiment is not equally present in everyone, no matter how talented they might be.

To instigate the creative conspiracy, team members must be completely engaged. In fact, lack of engagement is a big threat for effective teamwork: our research reveals that the most commonly cited problem in teams is "developing and sustaining motivation." This concern keeps 57 percent of people up at night, as they struggle to keep the collaborative effort strong and thriving. In this chapter, I outline the key reasons why people work and what motivates them and what demotivates them. I then take up the question of how to create the upbeat, engaged teams and then the question of what to do when a team member is disengaged.

Working for the Money or Working for the Meaning?

Intrinsic motivation comes from within, such as when we engage in an activity or hobby for the pure satisfaction of doing it. That is the motivation that my less-than-perfect-test-scores student had. *Extrinsic motivation* comes from external goals (such as when we do a job to get paid). Some people might say they work because they want to make a difference and because their work means something; this is intrinsic motivation. Other people might say they work because they need the money; this would be extrinsic motivation. Most people work in organizations for both reasons: they like what they do, but they also want to get paid.

However, there is an ego-driven disconnect in how people view their own teammates' motivation: most people believe they are motivated by intrinsic factors, but falsely assume that others are motivated by extrinsic factors. For example, 64 percent of attorneys report that *they* became a lawyer because it was their calling—an intrinsic motivation—but these same attorneys believe that 62 percent of their colleagues are motivated by money—an extrinsic motivation.

When we believe that others are extrinsically motivated, we tend to use material rewards to get them to do what we want them to do *to the exclusion of intrinsic rewards*. When we do this, however, a number of problems crop up. First, although the promise of external rewards can be temporarily satisfying, it ultimately requires a never-ending stream of extrinsic incentives to maintain that satisfaction. This is because people quickly adapt to extrinsic rewards and need more and more to feel satisfied. For example, suppose that you reward a team member with a bonus for meeting a difficult deadline. The next time you are involved in an engagement that has a tight deadline, the team member will expect a bonus reward and may even expect a reward larger than the previous one.

Second, over time, extrinsic motivation, in the absence of intrinsic affirmation, may very well undermine the employees' own interest in their job. This is because they may come to believe that they only work for the money or extrinsic reward. Finally, offering only extrinsic rewards results in less persistent and more superficial processing of information.

Maarten Vansteenkiste and his colleagues set up an interesting comparison of how intrinsic and extrinsic goals affect motivation and performance in two groups of schoolteachers. One group was told that they could save money by learning how to recycle (extrinsic motivation). The other was told they could learn how to teach their students the value of recycling and help with the problem of excess waste in their community (intrinsic motivation). Otherwise, there were no differences in how the groups were treated. Their performance was measured by a self-report, in which they answered honestly how much of the information given to them on recycling they had read, what the quality of their personal contribution in a group discussion about recycling with others was, and whether they took advantage of learning more about the subject by visiting a recycling plant or going to the library. The teachers given the intrinsic goal showed more autonomous motivation (i.e., they did tasks in a proactive fashion without being asked), persisted longer at difficult tasks, and processed information at a deeper level than those who were intrinsically motivated. Best of all, their performance was superior in the test task. The message: find a way to connect to the intrinsic interest of people—at least if you want them to self-motivate, persist, think deeply, and perform well! Managers often fail to take advantage of the power of praise in motivating others.

The More I Pay, the Less I Earn

Most people have heard the term *cognitive dissonance*, but they have not heard about the $20 versus $1 experiment. Leon Festinger, a psychologist and group expert, reasoned that if you had perfectly normal people do a really boring task, they could actually learn to love it—if you did not pay them very much. Sounds strange, right? Festinger had a large number of people turn wooden knobs—the most monotonous activity he could imagine—and he either paid them $20 or $1. Then, those folks had to tell another prospective participant how much they actually enjoyed doing the task. The $20 people said they hated the task and only did it for the money. However, the people who were paid only $1 actually grew to like the task! Why? The people who were paid only $1 could not tell themselves or anyone else that they did the task for the money, so they reasoned that they must be doing it because they loved it. *Cognitive dissonance* is the strong need for people to bring their beliefs into alignment with their behaviors: being paid only $1 for the boring task was disconcerting until the people doing it came to believe that they actually must like doing the task. By coming to such a conclusion, they resolved the dissonance. This also explains why people report loving volunteer work—clearly, they don't do it for the money.

Undermining Intrinsic Interest

What is the impact of rewarding people with money or goods to the exclusion of praise and recognition? If leaders only offer extrinsic rewards for great performance, might this eventually lead people to devalue their own intrinsic interest? For example, if someone enjoys public speaking or helping others for the pure pleasure of the activity, could offering this person a reward or cash payment lead (but not inevitably lead) that person to be less interested in the task itself over time? To examine this question, Teresa Amabile studied artists who worked either on commission or for no commission. Amabile reasoned that artists who are hired or paid to produce artwork (i.e., commissioned) would be extrinsically motivated, whereas those who were not under commission worked for the pure enjoyment and self-fulfillment of doing their craft—and therefore, were likely to be intrinsically motivated. And indeed, the least creative projects were those produced by artists who were hired or paid, suggesting that intrinsic motivation might be undermined by extrinsic rewards.

However, it is foolish to think that people don't want or need to be paid for their work! Employees' expected reward for high performance increases their feelings of performance pressure, which in turn is positively associated with their interest in their jobs. Performance pressure increases intrinsic interest and leads to greater creativity. People who receive rewards for high performance feel more pressure, but they also have more intrinsic interest and exhibit greater creativity.

I am not suggesting that people should not be paid or given extrinsic rewards. The key is to tie extrinsic rewards to creative idea generation. Indeed, when youngsters are given rewards for creative performance, their creativity increases in subsequent tasks. In one study, the promise of a reward for picture drawing increased creativity if children had previously generated novel uses for physical objects, with or without reward. However, the promise of reward did not increase creativity if the children had been rewarded for using objects in conventional ways. The takeaway is that training in creative thinking conveys a desire for creative performance that responds positively in the face of reward. This reward-creativity relationship is strengthened when kids are given training in divergent thinking and when creativity is emphasized. The same is true for adults. Reward promised for creativity increases college students' creative task performance. Employees who expected to be rewarded for high performance increased intrinsic job interest and made more creative suggestions at work. Apparently, when people expect rewards for performance, they are more self-determined.

It's Nurture, Not Nature

Claudia Mueller and Carol Dweck reasoned that even praise could backfire under the wrong conditions. Mueller and Dweck noted that there are at least two ways we can praise others—we can praise their innate, raw talent or we can praise their effort and resolve. For example, suppose that a manager makes a successful presentation for a client. We could either praise that manager's intelligence or we could highlight her exceptional motivation and effort. Intelligence and talent are largely immutable factors—not easy to take away, but also not easy to improve. They are fixed traits, so praise will not likely affect them. However, motivation and effort can be changed and improved. To test their hypothesis that praising intelligence might ultimately not be as motivating as praising effort, Mueller and Dweck studied 128 fifth-graders who were all tasked with solving ten Raven's Standard Progressive Matrices—nonverbal multiple choice measures of the reasoning that is linked to overall intelligence. Some students were praised for their intelligence (fixed trait); others were praised for their effort (malleable trait). The results of the study demonstrate that praise for intelligence had more negative consequences for students' achievement motivation than praise for effort. Students praised for intelligence cared more about performance goals than learning goals, compared with those praised for effort.

Failure was particularly problematic for those praised for intelligence: when they failed at a task, they displayed less task persistence, enjoyed it less, thought they had less ability, and ultimately performed worse than children praised for effort. Also, children praised for intelligence described it as a fixed trait more than children praised for hard work, who believed it to be subject to improvement. The bottom line: people want to believe that they can continually improve and thus, focusing on effort and persistence are key for motivating the creative team.

In another investigation, people were either intrinsically motivated (told to focus on their personal enjoyment of a task), test-focused (told they would be evaluated), or both (told to focus on their own enjoyment and that they would be evaluated). Before the task began, each group engaged in a noncreative or creative pre-task. The noncreative pre-task was simply substituting one word for another in a paragraph. In the creative pre-task, people read about a dream someone had, and then discussed the dream with an analyst. Those who had engaged in the creative pre-task and were purely intrinsically motivated were more creative, motivated, and remembered the information five days later.

Psychological Flow

When was the last time you were so completely immersed in doing something that you lost track of time and found yourself engaged, interested, and even joyful? Psychologist Mihalyi Csikszentmihalyi refers to this state as *psychological flow*. Flow is a feeling of spontaneous joy, even rapture, while performing a task. When people experience psychological flow, they are thoroughly immersed in what they are doing and focused on the present (as opposed to the past or future). Most important, they have struck a balance between boredom and stress, such that they are completely engaged and challenged but not overcome with anxiety and fear.

What are the conditions of psychological flow? The good news is that you don't need to be a theoretical physicist or ultra-distance runner to experience flow. Normal people can also experience flow if they:

- Have clear goals

- Get immediate feedback

- Experience deep concentration

- Focus on the present

- Take control

- Lose their ego

The critical thing is to balance the challenge that faces you with your skill level. If your level of skill is high and the challenge is also high, the conditions are right for flow. If the challenge exceeds your skill level, you will most likely feel anxiety. If you are highly skilled but not challenged, you will feel apathy and even boredom. Football analyst and former coach, Jon Gruden, experiences a state of mental flow every day. So excited about his work each day, Gruden plaintively asks, "Who needs sleep?" when he wakes at 3:15 and arrives at the office at 4 a.m. to watch game footage and practice films. When Gruden's mentor advised him that football is not everything, Gruden remarked, "It's my rhythm; it's the beat that I go to."

- *Clear goals*: First and foremost, the creative team needs to have absolutely clear goals. A sense of purpose and mission is paramount. For example, consider the creative team at Charter House Innovations, a furniture manufacturer that started out by providing interior furnishing to the quick service industry, such as McDonald's and Burger King. That led to hotels. Many furniture companies would be happy supplying hotels, but the company took it one step further and, in an unorthodox move, provided its own hotel to allow the team to maximize their creative potential. The team tested everything that would go in the guest rooms; it soon discovered that the beds were not comfortable, so Charter House then starting selling the beds that went into the hotels—after a team member tested several beds at her own home!

- *Immediate feedback*: For a state of team flow and complete engagement to occur, the team needs to get immediate feedback. Too often teams work without any indication of how they are doing, or feedback is delayed and muted. Conversely, teams who are positioned to get immediate results can quickly make revisions and changes. For example, to help Parkinson's disease patients, doctors teamed up with software developers at the University of Maryland to develop state-of-the-art technology that provides real-time feedback on a patient's progress. Because the software immediately translates a patient's movements onto a computer screen, doctors can alter the patient's therapy instantaneously.

- *Deep concentration*: The team needs to be able to concentrate deeply. It is important that the team not be distracted or diverted from their task. Complete engagement requires minimizing extraneous interruptions. For example, Harmon.ie, a software company in California, found that nearly 60 percent of employee work interruptions involved social networking, e-mail, or text messaging. To limit the distractions, some companies have instituted a No Facebook Friday rule to help teams focus on their work.

- *Focus on the present*: Too often, teams drift into discussions of the past or hypothetical discussions of the future. To experience true flow, teams need to live in the present. Larry Page, Google's CEO, keeps his staff focused on the tasks at hand by mandating that meetings run no longer than fifty minutes. Page says that having meetings go longer means having to allow for a bathroom break, which would break the focus of the here and now.

- *Control:* Teams experiencing psychological flow are in control rather than being controlled. Practically, this means they are empowered and have assumed responsibility for their work.

- *Loss of ego:* Finally, team members experiencing psychological flow have to lose their egos. The key is the mission and the goal, not their personal agendas. History was made in August 2012 when the US 4x100 relay team of Carmelita Jeter, Allyson Felix, Tianna Madison, and Bianca Knight raced to Olympic history, winning the gold medal and setting a new world record. Their success followed sixteen years of stunning failures by the US women's team. Tellingly, their coach explains the need for putting egos aside, "I don't care if they like each other, but for thirty-seven seconds, I need them to love each other."

Nurturing the Creative Team

If you could spend one hour doing something that could guarantee that your creative team would remain motivated and engaged what would you do? Consider the following.

Affirm Intrinsic Motivation

One method for instilling intrinsic interest is to affirm people's motivation and drive. For example, in one study, children were "paid" for doing artwork—all received an extrinsic reward. However, some children were also complimented for their motivation and inherent interest (e.g., "you must really feel good about working so hard"). Later, when all the children were given an opportunity to work in their free time, those whose intrinsic interest had been "validated" were more likely to choose to work on their art. Similarly, another investigation revealed that volunteers who are purely intrinsically motivated to help others have a stronger sense of purpose than volunteers who are offered extrinsic rewards for their work.

Recall Moments of Inspiration

Inspiration is a motivational state that energizes the actualization of creative ideas. One investigation showed how "peaks" in inspiration predict peaks in creative writing. Todd Thrash and his colleagues had two different groups of people write a simple paragraph. One group was told to write about a personal experience of inspiration—a time in their life where they felt particularly inspired. Another group was simply told to write about an experience in daily life. The groups were not differentiated in terms of personality or basic human motivation because it was randomly determined who was in each group. After completing this task, their performance in a job setting was examined. Those who had written about a personal experience of inspiration were judged to be more involved in their work and more motivated than those who had written about an experience of daily life. The effects of this groundbreaking investigation clearly indicate that merely reminiscing about moments of inspiration creates a self-fulfilling prophecy.

I often begin team meetings by asking members to talk about a moment in their lives when they were so inspired by someone or something that they might not be where they are right now without having experienced that moment. I ask them to share these stories of inspiration, and I have noticed a pattern. First, moments of inspiration often come at unexpected times. In other words, it is rarely the case that someone was looking for inspiration and then found it. Second, moments of inspiration often occur during a trough or low point in a person's life. One of my clients found his moment at the time he learned he had not passed the state bar exam. Third, moments of inspiration are usually not associated with receiving a monetary or extrinsic reward, but instead are associated with having a personal impact on others or the world. Ianthe Cupid's story provides a good example. When Cupid lost her leg in a horrific car accident, her future collapsed. Unable to work, she lost her job and her son suffered emotional trauma. She fell into the depths of despair. Then, in a flash of inspiration, she had the idea to bring joy to others by creating balloon sculptures. At first, she started making a few balloons to help pay the bills, but her passion was unstoppable, and soon her business, Cupid's Crafty Corner, was born.

Set Creativity Goals

Another way of instilling intrinsic interest is to give people a goal of creativity. In one investigation, the highest level of creativity occurred when people were given a goal to "be creative" and worked independently under the expectation of evaluation.

Highlight Superordinate Goals

A superordinate goal is one that is a higher-order mission—usually beyond the making of money and the achievement of fame. A superordinate goal is one that often unites and ignites people, organizations, and communities. If people aren't excited by the goal and the mission, then collaboration won't occur. People need a line of sight to the goal. They need the anticipation of an "opening night." Highly collaborative teams are often hard to tolerate because they are completely absorbed with their goals.

Goals are so important that they affect us even unconsciously. For example, in one investigation, a number of people on their way to work were shown a photo of a woman winning a race, while others were not. Those who were shown the photo performed better on a brainstorming task than those who did not see the winning-the-race photo. The message? Activating or priming unconscious goals increases people's subconscious need for achievement. Another study indicated that people who worked in a call center who had either a *conscious goal* or an *unconscious goal* were more productive in soliciting money from donors than those without goals.

What are *unconscious goals*? Any time we cannot point to the particular stimulus that affected us, we have most likely been influenced unconsciously. For example, in a study of men and women who had weight loss as a personal goal, one-third were led into a room that was set up as a sports psychology center filled with magazines about fitness and nutrition (diet focus); another third were led to a room that contained tempting, fattening foods—chocolate bars, cakes, and so on (food focus); and the final third were put into a control room filled with magazines about geography and the economy (control group). Upon leaving the waiting room, each participant was given a choice between a Twix bar and an apple. Participants in both the diet and the food rooms were more likely to choose the apple—as compared to those in the control room. Apparently, subliminal messages about either *vices or virtues* act to remind people of their ultimate goals and, in this sense, put them on high alert. Those in the food room were unconsciously reminded of the importance of resisting temptation, but those in the neutral room were the most likely to slip away from their ultimate goals.

Make It Personal

The greater the level of personal involvement a person has in a task or mission, the more engaging the goal is. Ideally, the goal should be connected to the personal identity of the individuals involved. *Self-identity* is how a person defines himself. People want to be connected to their goal. They want to feel inspired by it. One investigation of female engineers found that those who identified both with women *and* engineers were more creative in designing a product for female users than those who did not identify with either group.

Drama Kings and Queens

Have you ever wondered how your moods affect your motivation? And your creativity? And how your mood affects those of people around you? In general, the research suggests that positive mood is associated with greater creativity. Indeed, there is a strong, positive linear relationship between positive mood and creativity. Perhaps the most persuasive evidence is the result of a meta-analysis of sixty-two experimental and ten nonexperimental studies that evaluated the relationship between mood and creativity. The results indicate that positive mood enhances creativity, and the strength of the effect is contingent on the comparative or referent mood state. In other words, if you are naturally cheerful, then positive mood won't have as much of an impact as it would for a person who is usually neutral.

If you are curious about your own moods, think about which of the following words describe you most accurately:

interested	upset	scared	proud	ashamed
distressed	strong	hostile	irritable	inspired
excited	guilty	enthusiastic	alert	nervous
determined	attentive	jittery	active	afraid

Interested, excited, strong, enthusiastic, proud, alert, inspired, determined, active, and *attentive* indicate positive mood. Conversely, *distressed, upset, guilty, scared, hostile, irritable, ashamed, nervous, jittery,* and *afraid* all indicate negative mood. In my research with Cameron Anderson at the University of California, Berkeley, we measured the chronic (daily) moods of people engaged in conflict and negotiations using the words above. We found that powerful negotiators were particularly contagious—meaning that their moods spilled over to affect those they were dealing with. In addition, their moods affected whether they were able to craft creative win-win agreements in complex negotiations. In short, unhappy leaders were more likely to negatively rub off on others. The implications for creative collaboration are pretty dramatic: mood undeniably affects mental processing, and our moods have a measurable impact on others. Further, the more power, status, and influence we have, the more contagious we are with regard to our mood. Some leaders are keenly aware of how much their personal state of mind and mood affects their employees. For example, Gary Burnison, CEO of

Korn/Ferry International, the world's largest executive recruiting firm, noticed that when he was having what he calls a "gray day," his employees started to wonder if they should be concerned too. To compensate, Burnison began to pay more attention to how he talked and conveyed messages to employees in meetings. As a start, he used fewer PowerPoint slides, which he thinks did not come across as positive, and instead concentrated on conveying a positive tone when talking to his staff. Burnison's intuitions are spot-on. Indeed, people who witness authority figures acting in a rude way are less creative. And unbridled anger is as injurious as "smoking a pack of cigarettes each day." Moreover, witnessing rudeness in one's organization decreases citizenship behaviors and increases dysfunctional ideation (negative, ruminating thoughts). The reason is that rude people put most of us in a bad mood.

Cultivating a positive workplace pays off. In another study of 222 employees in seven companies, measured positive affect was correlated with greater creativity in an organization. Positive affect is a precursor to creative thought, and often the incubation period is up to two days. That means that the cognitive-neural pathways stimulated by mood last for over forty-eight hours. Stated another way: if you are in a positive mood on Monday, you might fully expect to have a creative breakthrough on Wednesday!

In another investigation, temporary work groups were induced to experience a positive, neutral, or negative mood before engaging in a creative production task. Positive mood increased creative performance as well as the efficiency of implementation, but negative mood had no effect. Positive moods increased the task focus of the groups. People who are led to be in a positive mood generate more original ideas than people who are in a neutral mood. Similarly, people who have been offered positive (as opposed to negative) feedback are more likely to give helpful hints to others.

Yet, does negative mood always adversely affect creativity? No. Negative moods stimulate creativity under certain conditions. For example, groups of people in negative moods generated more creative advertising slogans than groups in positive moods. In this case, the key driver was persistence—people in negative moods persisted longer. And positive mood may not help teams perform well in noncreative tasks, such as solving problems and completing logical syllogisms. For example, people in positive moods are more likely to select an unqualified conclusion, spend less time on a task, diagram the key relationships of a problem less thoroughly, and perform less well on the completion of a syllogism. Below, we draw a distinction between activating and deactivating moods and make the point that negative moods that increase arousal might very well spur creativity

In general, however, the preponderance of evidence suggests that positive mood increases creativity. What are the implications for the creative conspiracy? Clearly, there are benefits to positive mood. But I do not advocate that people paint on a fake smile. Feigned affect and false smiles may very well be more damaging than a heartfelt negative display of emotion. A study of feigned affect among bank tellers revealed that over time, this led to worse customer relationships!

The Mere Exposure Effect

The more we see something or spend time with someone—even things and people we don't like—the more we come to like them. Psychologists refer to this as the *mere exposure effect*. The mere exposure effect has been demonstrated with nearly everything under the sun—including words, paintings, pictures of faces, geometric figures, sounds and people—whether we initially like them or not! The mere exposure effect takes place without conscious thought and very quickly. What's the implication for creative teamwork? Simple: doing a particular task leads to liking it more and more. Being around familiar people leads to liking them more and more. Think of it as a kind of self-fulfilling, positive-mood prophecy!

One key to positive mood then is to make some things familiar. Happy people are drawn to tasks that involve creativity. Even more notable, when happy people are threatened with a negative mood, they exhibit even greater *cognitive flexibility*—they open their minds to think about new ways to look at the situation. Happy people effectively transform tasks so as to maintain their positive mood and their high interest level. In studies of negotiation and creative problem-solving people who are happy or in an otherwise good mood are more likely to generate creative, nonobvious solutions.

Chilling Out Is Not a Good Idea

Some moods are *activating*, in the sense that they prepare one for behavior and action (e.g., anger, fear, happiness, elation). Other moods are *deactivating*, meaning that they do not prepare one for action states (e.g., sadness, depression, relaxation, serenity). Intuitively, we might think that relaxation would lead to greater creativity. However, when people are relaxed or "chilled out," they are not actually very creative. Activation can be thought of like your heart rate. Excitement is positive and activating and increases our heart rate. Relaxation is positive, but deactivating—it decreases our heart rate. Activating moods lead to more creative ideas and more original ideas than do deactivating moods. There are different reasons why both positive and negative activating moods increase creativity. The reason positive activating moods increase creativity is that positive moods increase cognitive flexibility (i.e., broaden one's thinking). In other words, people in an active, positive mood think of more solutions to problems and challenges. The reason negative activating moods increase creativity is that negative moods increase persistence. In other words, people in an active, negative mood persist more vigorously and try harder.

Not surprisingly, nearly any kind of physical activity can lead to an activating mind-set. I know of one professor who begins each class by asking students to stand up and walk around. Mark Rittenberg, CEO of the consulting firm of Corporate Scenes, punctuates his hour-long presentations with a vigorous chanting exercise at the halfway point. In short, moving and other physical activity are activating. Moreover, they have life-changing effects on our mood and even our life span! So, don't stop moving! Women who sat six hours or more per day increased their risk of death by 37 percent over a thirteen-year period compared with people who sat fewer than three hours a day. Men who sat more than six hours per day increased their death risk by 18 percent over thirteen years compared with men who sat for fewer than three hours a day. It is for this reason that many companies now offer yoga, swimming, running, weight training, and cycling programs as an integral part of the workday. The key to staying active is recovery. What's the best recovery? Sleep! In Silicon Valley, we see examples of tech workers who sleep with devices that measure their REM, ingest low-glycemic food, and have dumped their desk chairs in favor of standing or treadmill desks. When they brainstorm, they bypass the conference room and go for a walk. Innovative companies are supporting their creative tech teams and offer free gym memberships, on-site gyms, nap pods, and hammocks—not to mention onsite chefs who produce healthy gourmet meals. Google offers onsite physical therapists, masseuses, and chiropractors along with gyms and fitness classes. Biometric screening measures blood pressure, cholesterol, and health apps. Similarly, Facebook features yoga and boot camp classes, personal trainers, nutritionists, and, of course, health dashboards for tracking body signals. Keith Rabois, COO of Square, relies on a Zeo sleep monitor to pace his day, and his team checks his sleep score before pitching him radical innovations.

A Mind in Motion Stays in Motion . . .

My colleagues and I conducted a series of studies that suggest that when it comes to creativity, it is more conducive to be in an activating mood than a deactivating mood. Positive moods can increase creativity when they promote safe work environments and increase creative cognition. Negative moods can increase creativity when they signal an aversive environment that motivates flexible thinking. What's interesting about activating versus deactivating states is that pleasant, soothing things tend to calm us down and deactivate us; but boring, tedious, annoying things tend to make us search for ways to activate a more pleasant state. For example, in one of our studies, we asked people to list two activities that they would perform to increase their creative thinking. Not surprisingly, most people believe that engaging in activities that induce positive-deactivating moods (pleasant moods) increase creativity more than do activities that induce positive-acting moods and negative moods. Participants showed a strong bias toward positive-deactivating activities (57 percent) followed by positive-activating (32 percent) and negative-activating (10 percent) and negative-deactivating (1 percent). Only 42 percent of participants chose to engage in an activating activity over a deactivating activity. Moreover, negative-activating activities were underutilized. These (faulty) beliefs lead people to engage in deactivating activities that fail to enhance creativity over positive- or negative-activating activities.

Armed with these findings, we then attempted to discover how certain types of corporate off-sites might affect creativity. One group of business executives was told to tell a story about an experience in which they felt proud. Another group of executives was told to tell a story about a time in which they were embarrassed. Whereas the majority of participants believed that talking about a moment of pride would result in greater creativity (88 percent) than talking about an embarrassing moment (12 percent), the actual results proved them wrong. Executives who shared embarrassing stories generated 26 percent more creative ideas than did those who shared proud stories! The reason is that embarrassing stories do two things: they are activating in that people laugh and get excited and they also involve some risk because we make ourselves vulnerable.

A Business Case for Happiness

So far, we've talked about mood—temporary emotional states that impact our own behavior and others'. But what about chronic, more enduring states—such as our overall level of happiness, and, for that matter, our outlook on life? How do they impact performance and creativity?

Before reading further, take the following true/false quiz:

1. Happy people are more productive at work than unhappy people.

2. Happy people have better immune systems and are less likely to get sick than unhappy people.

3. Happy people live longer and have better lives than unhappy people.

4. Happy people have more money and other material resources than unhappy people.

5. In general, positive mood is conducive to creativity and innovation.

Answer key: 1. True, 2. True, 3. True, 4. False, 5. True

If you are surprised by any of the answers, you, like many people, have probably thought that happiness is nice—kind of like a luxury—but not really a necessity. In fact, however, happiness has benefits that are much greater than just good mood. Happy people live longer and are less likely to suffer from debilitating diseases. Happy people are less likely to get sick and they have better immune systems. Happy people perform better at work. Happy doctors have higher patient satisfaction scores, and their patients live longer. Happy people are absent less often from work and are more likely to engage in random acts of kindness and organizational citizenship behaviors. Happy people have better social relationships. They are more likely to get married, stay married, and have happy marriages. In contrast, unhappy people are absent more from work and change jobs more often. They are less cooperative and less helpful. They perform worse at work. And they negatively affect the loyalty of their customers and clients.

But, just what is happiness? Happiness is your *enduring level of well-being*. It is how you feel in general (for the past several months). If you are curious as to how you stack up to most Americans, Michael Fordyce's Emotions Questionnaire asks, in general, how happy or unhappy do you usually feel? Using a ten-point scale, ranging from 1 (extremely unhappy; i.e., utterly depressed and completely down) to 10 (extremely happy; i.e., ecstatic, joyous, fantastic), where would you rate yourself? The average US person is about a 6.92 (mildly happy, feeling fairly good, and somewhat cheerful). Similarly, most people feel happy about 54 percent of the time; they feel unhappy 20 percent of the time and neutral about 26 percent of the time.

In my research with team leaders, the average level of subjective well-being (i.e., *how satisfied are you with your life?*) is 5.43 on a seven-point scale (1 = very dissatisfied; 7 = very satisfied).

Another widely researched measure is Sonja Lyubomirsky and Heidi Lepper's General Happiness scale:

- In general, I consider myself (not a very happy person vs. a very happy person)

- Compared to most of my peers, I consider myself (less happy vs. very happy)

- Some people are generally very happy. They enjoy life regardless of what is going on, getting the most out of everything. To what extent does this characterization describe you? (not at all vs. a great deal)

- Some people are generally not very happy. Although they are not depressed, they never seem to as happy as they might be. To what extent does this characterization describe you? (less happy vs. more happy)

You can answer each of the statements above on a 1–7 scale. To score, total your answers and divide by 4. The average for adult Americans is 4.8. Two-thirds of people score between 3.8 and 5.8.

What are the implications for the creative conspiracy? Take the time to find out what the chronic level of happiness and well-being of your team is. If it is on the low side, don't despair! Yes, it is true that some of our enduring level of happiness is rather fixed or immutable, but a great deal of it is highly subject to the intentional activities that we consciously choose to engage in. This means that we can change our enduring level of happiness by thinking more deliberately about what we want to invest our time in.

Bad Genes or Bad Attitude?

At this point, you are probably wondering whether happiness is mostly due to nature or nurture. Do we inherit happiness or do we fall into or out of it as a function of our circumstances? The answer is, both. First the bad news: about 40 to 50 percent of your chronic level of happiness is inherited. Thus, if mom or dad was a curmudgeon, then there is nothing you can do about it—you got some of their genes! Now the good news: 20 to 30 percent of your chronic level of happiness is determined by your conscious activities—the behaviors and choices that you make on a daily level dramatically affect your enduring level of well-being. In one powerful class assignment, Marty Seligman of the University of Pennsylvania, told his students to do one of two things: go out and enjoy themselves or help somebody. Specifically, one group was instructed to enjoy themselves (i.e., party, celebrate, go out on the town); another group was told to engage in a philanthropic activity (i.e., use their skills to help somebody, such as offering to tutor a struggling student or volunteer at a local charity). The students then wrote about how they felt afterward. The results were life-changing. Initially, both groups were equally happy. However, as soon as one week and even one month later, the students who had helped others were happier than those who simply engaged in a pleasurable activity. The positive effects of the philanthropic activities were much longer-lasting. Bottom line: improving our enduring level of happiness involves more than simply engaging in the good life or pleasures; rather, it involves using our unique strengths to help others and our teams.

The problem is that most people falsely assume that acquiring material goods and making more money will improve their happiness. Material wealth and income *do* improve happiness, but only up to a point. To a person living below the poverty line and under stress about how to pay bills, making more money dramatically improves happiness. However, once people reach a moderate level of income, increasing income after that does not buy more happiness. Even people who win multimillion-dollar lotteries eventually return to their set point, chronic level of pre-lottery-win happiness. A study of twenty-two lottery winners proved that even though they won a fortune, they were not happy and satisfied living their "everyday" lives.

Why? The answer lies in what is known as the *hedonic treadmill*. As we make more money, it feels good initially, but then we quickly adapt to our new level of income and, in fact, feel that we must keep increasing our income to keep up. The more money you make, the more money you spend, but you're not necessarily happier. Studies of shopping and product purchases also reveal that new purchases do increase our level of well-being—for about ten to fourteen days. Then we adapt, meaning the new dining room table is—well, no longer new. The new car now has a scratch on it, and our neighbor just bought a nicer model. In the introduction of his book *Enough*, investing legend and Vanguard founder John Bogle relays the following story: "At a party given by a billionaire on Shelter Island, Kurt Vonnegut informs his pal, Joseph Heller, that their host, a hedge fund manager, had made more money in a single day than Heller had earned from his wildly popular novel *Catch-22* over its whole history. Heller responds, 'Yes, but I have something he will never have . . . enough.'"

The mistake that we see most people make is that they are chasing temporary happiness instead of enduring happiness. What are the keys to enduring happiness?

Self-reflecting about happy events: People who think about happy life events for eight minutes every day for three days are significantly happier than those who don't. These effects last up to four weeks!

Meaningful conversations: People who have a deep, meaningful conversation with someone at least once per week are happier than those who talk about superficial interests.

Physical activity: People who engage in aerobic activity increase not only their physical health, but improve their long-term moods. Dancing improves happiness. Jumping jacks improve happiness. Playing Boggle, Taboo, or charades or other energetic games improves happiness. Rapidly and energetically recounting a story to friends improves happiness.

Envisioning happiness: People who brainstorm their top ten dream vacation destinations, the fifteen favorite people in your life, and set their screen saver to scroll through inspirational quotes are happier.

Gifting: People who give something to others are happier.

The power of positive mood has gained recognition as an iPhone app. For $1.99, you can download the Live Happy app and be reminded of scientifically proven benefits of positive psychology. The app, designed by psychologist Sonja Lyubomirsky, is a buddy that prompts you to engage in positive activities, such as looking at a photo of your child or expressing your gratitude to a coworker.

Chapter Capstone

We've examined two key types of motivation—intrinsic and extrinsic. Intrinsic motivation comes from within and it sustains us and motivates us to persist and be creative. Extrinsic motivation, in comparison, is based on rewards. We've seen how using extrinsic rewards to the exclusion of intrinsic motivation can eventually undermine people's motivation and ultimately hurt their performance—although this is in no way an argument that we should start praising people and freezing their salaries. However, most leaders miss key opportunities to affirm intrinsic interest because they falsely believe that others are purely extrinsically motivated. We reviewed the model of psychological flow—a state in which people are so involved in their tasks that the act of doing the task is its own reward—and have considered some concrete suggestions for creating conditions for psychological flow in creative teams and instilling intrinsic interest in people. We examined how positive mood affects creativity and we made a strong business case for happiness. Finally, I hope this chapter has dispelled the notion that happiness is something that a person falls into; rather, we can cultivate happiness by choosing to invest our time and energy in pursuits that sustain ourselves and our teams.

CHAPTER 6

Transforming Conflict into Creativity

Bono is a superstar in the music world. In 2011, he wrote the music and lyrics for the musical *Spider Man: Turn Off the Dark*—at $75 million dollars, the most expensive show ever produced on Broadway. However, Bono is not used to failure. And that was a big problem when *Spider Man* was declared a spectacular flop in early reviews. Bono and his U2 bandmate, The Edge, first began collaborating with renowned director Julie Taymor on the music for the show in 2002. But Bono came to regret this collaboration. "The hours and weeks and months . . . If we thought it would take this long, there is not a chance on earth we would have done it." However, throughout the collaboration, Bono retained faith in Taymor and her talent. But when the show opened in preview, critics savaged its plot as "incoherent" and "boring," which cut Bono to the core. In hindsight, Bono wishes he had spoken up about his doubts. However, he self-silenced because he feared that Taymor would walk out of the show if he criticized her—he felt that he could not be open with her.

The opening example reveals how people—even superstars—are terribly afraid of conflict. They don't want to rock the boat, even when millions of dollars are on the line and their inner voice is screaming for them to say something. As it turns out, *Spider*

Man recovered from its early failures and has since been breaking box office records. So this is also a case in point that teams can recover from early failures—if they are willing to engage in the process of healthy conflict.

Conflict in a team is inevitable. But recognizing it and making it work for you in a team is anything but easy. Most people don't like conflict and so they don't want to deal with it; and when they do, they immediately want to extinguish it. So, repeat after me: *conflict is a sign of a high-performing team.* Now, say it like you mean it!

When I was a young assistant professor at the University of Washington, one of my dearest colleagues was John Gottman; you may know him as the world-renowned marriage and parenting researcher. In his long-term, cutting-edge studies, Gottman found that the couples with the strongest marriages—the ones that endure over time—are the couples that fight. Yes, that's right. They fight; they don't avoid conflict. However, there is a particular *way* these couples fight. They fight *fairly*. For example, consider the difference between one partner saying, "*I don't trust you. You are a creep!*" versus, "*I am really angry and I feel that I have lost trust!*" The first example is a personal attack; one spouse calls the other a name ("creep"). In the second example, the spouse has communicated anger *without* a personal attack. For Gottman, one of the keys to a successful marriage is the separation of pure anger from personal attacks. I argue that there is a parallel for teams—people in teams spend a lot of time with each other and get in each other's way, just as the partners in a long-term relationship.

Similarly, in my studies of negotiation, I have discovered that win-win outcomes result when negotiators are tough, ask penetrating questions, drill down for the core issues, and are hard on the problem, not the people. In fact, when negotiators are too polite and avoid sensitive topics, they are more likely to settle upon lose-lose outcomes.

In one of my research projects with Erika Peterson, we observed how teams of friends negotiate and compared them with teams composed of strangers. At first blush, it would seem that teams of friends would have a distinct advantage over teams composed of people who had no working relationship. Well, we were wrong. Teams of friends were excessively preoccupied about their relationships, and this interfered with their ability to focus on the task of negotiating. Things got even worse when the friends needed to depend on one other for information and when they had to report to a boss. In this case, teams composed of complete strangers actually reached more win-win agreements than did the teams of friends. Excessive concern for the relationship effectively shut down the ability of the teams to search for and integrate valuable information. Being polite is not conducive to the creative crafting of win-win negotiations.

The same is true for creative teamwork. In a study of seventy-one IT project teams, creativity was highest at moderate levels of *task conflict*—differences and disagreements on ideas, opinions, and interpretations of facts within the team. In contrast, *relationship conflict* deals with interpersonal conflict between the people in the group rather than the task they are working on. The importance of a moderate amount of task conflict in a team is particularly important when the group is in an early phase. Thus, it is important to set the stage for disagreement early on in the life of a team.

Fear of Conflict

Unfortunately, most people, particularly Americans, are afraid of conflict. Why? There are two major reasons.

First, we don't know how to separate the people from the problem. When we are attacked or threatened, our defense systems go into overdrive, and we usually respond by attacking the person who attacked us. This, of course, leads to an escalating spiral of tensions. To combat this pattern, we need some lessons on how to attack the *problem*, not the *person*. One of my colleagues has an effective behavioral technique for dealing with conflict. Whenever she feels that someone is attacking her, she takes one small step to the side and visualizes the angry words from the attacker going over her shoulder, rather than in her face.

Apparently, she is onto something big. My colleague Roderick Swaab at INSEAD suspected that visual contact between men who are on opposite sides of a negotiation table would lead to more aggression than if these men did not have visual access to each other. So, Swaab had men negotiate with either direct visual contact or no visual contact. All men then engaged in the same negotiation, with the same stakes, bottom lines, and so on, to ensure that any differences in the negotiated outcomes would not be due to economic factors, but rather psychological factors. As it turned out, the men who were in visual contact experienced an increase in testosterone levels.

Apparently, this physiological effect occurs because people, and men in particular, are hardwired to go into fight mode when they face a competitor. So, men who had direct visual contact essentially initiated an animal-stare-down with one another, tensions rising. The increases in testosterone led to more aggressive behavior and less mutually beneficial, creative outcomes. In contrast, the absence of direct visual contact paved the path toward more mutually beneficial agreements.

A second reason we avoid conflict is that we want to be liked. In this regard, most people subconsciously (and, as it turns out, mistakenly) assume that if they initiate conflict, others won't like them.

Code Cracking

Because of the inherent difficulties in navigating conflict, people often use indirect forms of communication rather than direct communication to convey what they mean. I refer to the use of indirect communication in conflict as *conflict code*. Conflict code is like a different language—if you don't know the code, something is certainly going to be lost in interpretation. The problem with using conflict code is that people on the receiving end are required to engage in several mental contortions to attempt to figure out what the other person means. This requires a lot of needless information processing, and receivers become exasperated or just downright confused. In short, they don't know how to crack the code. For example, consider a conflict in a work group in which one person really wants "Dan" to leave the team. There are at least nine different ways to communicate this to Dan, ranging from the blunt and direct to the nuanced and indirect:

1. Dan, leave the project team.

2. Dan, we're wondering whether it might be best if you left the team.

3. Dan, we're thinking that we don't need your involvement in the team at this point.

4. Dan, we're wondering if your talents might be best utilized elsewhere.

5. Dan, we're thinking that the team is ahead of schedule and does not require its original staffing.

6. Dan, have you thought about involving yourself in some of the new projects and lessening your involvement in others?

7. Dan, many of the original projects are being reconfigured; yours might be one that is affected.

8. Dan, the team has been able to take on the project, thanks to your early involvement.

9. Dan, we were hoping you would help us out with some of these new projects.

The first statement is direct and to the point; the subsequent statements are increasingly indirect, requiring Dan to have greater and greater insight into the unspoken intentions of the speaker. We have found that most people prefer to receive direct communication, but (falsely) believe that others are best served by using indirect, softer messages. Thus, there is a double standard.

According to Kellogg professor Vicki Medvec, *the illusion of transparency* is the belief that our thoughts, feelings, and intentions are clearer than they actually are. Most people believe that they are better communicators than they really are. Similarly, most people believe that their intentions and goals are more apparent than is actually the case. The illusion of transparency leads to problems for creative collaboration when team members are confused about what others are communicating. As a case in point, consider the failed launch of the *Mars Climate Orbiter* in 1999, in which a failure to communicate cost NASA's Jet Propulsion Laboratory (JPL) $125 million. Lockheed Martin engineers sent the orbiter's navigation information to JPL in Pasadena using the English measurement—*pounds of force*. But JPL had programmed its computers to calculate orbital navigation parameters and thruster firings using metric *newtons of force*. Neither group saw this problem because they thought their communications were transparent!

The remedy is to use more direct forms of communication and constantly check your understanding. Successful collaboration requires that people be in a heightened state of communication. In my own work with clients and students, I have gotten into the habit of summarizing what I think we have agreed to and have repeatedly found that my understanding is sometimes sorely lacking. Fortunately, this is quickly rectified at the end of the conversation, but could create a collaboration nightmare if too much time has passed!

The Mismanagement of Agreement

As a native Texan, since the first time I heard the fateful story of Jerry Harvey's trip to Abilene, I have been wary of team decision making. While spending quality time with his in-laws and extended family in Coleman, Texas, one hot July day, management scientist Jerry Harvey witnessed a curious group dysfunction. Things started very innocently. Everybody was enjoying cold lemonade and the company of family on the porch. Suddenly, someone casually suggested that the entire family could drive to Abilene for ice cream. Despite the fact that Abilene was over fifty miles away and the only means of transportation was an unairconditioned car, the family members each nodded their heads slowly, saying they thought the idea was just fine. Several hours later, after a sweat-soaked crammed car ride across the Texas desert, the family returned to the comfort of their porch. After a long silence, somebody finally said, "That was fun . . ." That apparently was the last straw. One person finally spoke up and said, "Actually I was miserable." Eventually everybody confessed that they had thought taking the drive was a terrible idea and didn't want to go at all, but didn't want to rock the boat. Why didn't they say anything hours earlier—before packing into the car and driving? According to Harvey, everyone falsely assumed that others wanted to go—a form of *pluralistic ignorance*. If the creative team does not speak up, they are also doomed to make arduous trips to Abilene.

Harvey's experience reveals the common tendency for groups to make less-than-optimal decisions. It also points to the fact that people in teams don't speak up and challenge one another because they are afraid of rocking the boat. When it comes to creative thinking, the last thing we want is to drive to Abilene. The group would have been much better off enjoying the porch and the lemonade. Yet so often, organizations and teams repress their reservations, agree for the sake of avoiding feared conflict, and end up with a less-than-rewarding process—and often a collectively disastrous decision.

Neutralizing Alpha-Dominant People

Another reason teams often experience conflict is that people are unhappy with the allocation of the scarcest of team resources: time. The next time you go to a team meeting, surreptitiously get out a sheet of paper and bring a watch. Record who talks and for how long, and at the end of the meeting, add up how many minutes each person had the floor. If your meetings are anything like the hundreds studied by management scientists, you probably noticed that a minority of people did a majority of the talking. The rest of the folks did not get a word in edgewise!

This problem is known as the *uneven communication problem*. There are a few dominant people in most groups who control and monopolize the discussion. For example, in a typical four-person group, two people do 62 percent of the talking. In a six-person group, three people do 70 percent of the talking; and in an eight-person group, three people do 70 percent of the talking. The topper is that the dominant people do not realize this. In fact, they vehemently argue that the meetings are egalitarian. They lack self-awareness.

The question becomes: Why are the rest of us here? A dysfunctional self-fulfilling prophecy starts to unfold week after week in these meetings: the dominant people begin to feel that the silent people are unprepared or simply don't have any opinions, so they dominate more; similarly, the quiet folks feel that it is futile to try to be heard, so they stop trying. Left unchecked, this creates a self-perpetuating doom loop in the group. Team members may blame one another for the unsatisfactory team meeting. In order to get the most out of collaboration, it is important to neutralize the too-dominant people and encourage the too-submissive people. However, just saying, "Shut up" or "Speak up" does not work. We need a more effective technique.

How can teams and team leaders deal with the uneven communication problem? Well, admonishing people to be brief, let others talk, or simply to monitor themselves is ineffective. To neutralize the dominant personalities in any group—I call this *forced democracy*—I offer three techniques: brainwriting, nominal group technique (NGT), and cyberstorming. We mentioned some of these very briefly in chapter 2—let's take a closer look here.

Brainwriting

Let's get this straight: *brainwriting is not brainstorming*. Brainwriting is the simultaneous written generation of ideas. I use two simple rules in my work with teams: (1) no guessing and (2) no confessions. In practical terms, this means that no one can attempt to determine who came up with what idea, nor can people confess which idea they authored. Rather, all ideas are anonymous. It is my custom to arrive at a brainwriting session with several hundred index cards and make it clear that each idea should be written on its own card in (reasonably!) legible writing. I pass out a generous number of cards. I like to keep brainwriting episodes short, no longer than ten minutes at a stretch—even five minutes works well. After the brainwriting episode, I collect all the cards and post them on a wall or, if a wall is not available, I have the group members sort them into piles according to general themes or similarity. The next step is to vote on which ideas people like the most. I like to do the voting privately; if possible, by having people put stickers on their favorite ideas. If they are milling about in a large enough group, this provides a reasonable amount of anonymity. Otherwise, the cards can be given a letter or number and people can submit votes privately, indicating which idea cards they like the most.

Once the votes are added up, I flag the top four to six ideas. At this point, I often like to spontaneously form four to six groups and give each group a flip chart and twenty minutes to take that idea to the "next level." Each group then has five minutes to present the flip chart with their results to the rest of the group. I typically pass the index cards around and ask everyone to give a piece of advice or suggestion feedback to each group. The groups now have a stack of cards to use to further refine their ideas.

Using this iterative technique, brainwriting can be woven into interactive team meetings in a way that keeps everyone engaged. The group is constantly cycling between independent idea generation, posting, voting, elaborating, and refining. I've rarely encountered teams that are resistant to brainwriting. Most people are amazed at how greatly the volume of ideas is increased. If I feel that I can get away with it, I provide everybody in a team with a toy water pistol and instruct them to shoot anyone who violates the rules (i.e., no confessions, no guessing).

The evidence for the effectiveness of brainwriting is indisputable. Groups that use brainwriting are dramatically more productive in terms of generating ideas than groups that don't use brainwriting and even groups that use brainstorming. Brainwriting can be made even more effective when group members carefully discuss the ideas exchanged by members (attention) and when they reflect on these ideas (incubation).

Whereas most companies use brainstorming, few, if any, use brainwriting. Yet the scientific evidence of its effectiveness is overwhelming. I worked with one company whose brainstorming goal was to try to get its customers to want to change their motor oil more often. I thought about the cheap plastic sticker on my windshield . . . and got intrigued. I passed out over 250 index cards to the thirty attendees and asked them to write down ideas, and set aside issues of acceptability, cost, and feasibility. I set the clock for ten minutes of brainwriting and collected over 400 cards. We shuffled the cards and gave each table a stack of cards to sort into common themes in fifteen minutes. Each table summarized the themes on a flip chart. Then, we did a round of voting and found five pockets of excitement. Over the next forty-five minutes, we formed five teams to take each of those ideas to the next level and be ready to make a ten-minute presentation. Following the presentations, everybody was encouraged to write a tip card to further expand that idea, still following the no-guessing and no-confessions policy. We then rotated the team members within each of the groups to inject new perspectives as ideas were being refined. At the end of the session, there were five new, exciting ideas that emerged that everyone felt ownership of. These ideas were taken to upper management, funded, and ultimately acted on.

Nominal Group Technique (NGT)

The nominal group technique is a lot like brainwriting. However, it is a more extreme version, in which people, rather than working in interactive groups, perform completely independently (i.e., in a *nominal group*) on a task or creative challenge, after which their responses or output are pooled. For this reason, NGT is ideally suited for distance-challenged groups that don't have the luxury of face-to-face time.

The research findings overwhelmingly indicate that nominal groups outperform interactive groups at brainstorming tasks, particularly when the problem is specialized. Yet companies still favor group interaction for some reason. Some argue that groups are better at selecting ideas, or that real group work is more satisfying. However, there is no scientific support for this. Not only do nominal groups outperform real groups in terms of idea generation, they are just as likely to select superior ideas and are just as satisfied with the process as interactive groups. This question was further examined in a study in which interactive groups were compared with nominal groups: nominal groups generated more ideas, more original ideas, and were more likely to select original ideas than interactive brainstormers. Yet, the myth of the superiority of real group work lives on!

Cyberstorming

Cyberstorming—also known as electronic brainstorming—emerged when companies and teams realized that people can interact meaningfully via computers. In a cyberstorming session, members are not colocated, but they are connected via computer or Internet. In an electronic brainstorming session (EBS), team members are in the same room, but instead of verbalizing ideas (and competing for the floor)—group members simply type their ideas into a database that is immediately displayed on a large screen. Cyberstorming and electronic brainstorming elegantly solve the problem of *production blocking*—the interference that occurs when team members compete with one another to speak at the same time. There is nothing to prevent members from verbalizing ideas, but only those that get entered are recorded. This means that the overly dominant personalities do not usurp the meeting. Cyberstorming also provides a cognitive stimulus to team members. Because the ideas are immediately displayed, they can spur new ideas in members reading the screen display. Another advantage is that members' ideas are anonymous.

Companies that are faced with distance-teamwork challenges might find a serendipitous effect with cyberstorming, as it can either be anonymous or not. There is some evidence that more controversial ideas are produced by members of anonymous electronic groups than by members of nonanonymous groups. Moreover, anonymous electronic groups produce fewer redundant ideas than do non-anonymous electronic groups.

Cyberstorming works because it overcomes the limitations of face-to-face (FTF) brainstorming—there is no one who can dominate a discussion, criticize ideas, talk too long, or interrupt. Groups using electronic brainstorming outperform both FTF brainstorming groups and nominal groups because they act not as a group, but as a collection of individuals who interact with an evolving set of ideas rather than with other people. One concern with EBS is information overload. In short, people may feel overwhelmed because they have to contribute ideas and also monitor ideas that other members are simultaneously contributing. To be sure, there is multitasking involved because participants are not only expected to contribute ideas but also must read the ideas that are fast emerging in the group. However, compared with face-to-face brainstorming sessions in which any number of factors can derail brainstorming, electronic groups are task focused.

In short, brainwriting, nominal group technique, and cyberstorming are all, hands down, superior to the typical face-to-face team meeting, although nominal brainstorming groups seem to have the edge. One investigation compared the quality of ideas generated by four different types of team configurations— nominal groups, interactive groups, EBS-anonymous groups, and EBS-nonanonymous groups—and found that, overall, nominal brainstorming groups generated ideas at least as good, if not better, than EBS groups. Another investigation designed a brainstorming application that used an interactive table and a large wall display and compared the results to traditional brainstorming. The electronic brainstorming application resulted in better-quality ideas than traditional FTF brainstorming. Yet, faulty beliefs about the efficacy of FTF brainstorming still exist. Organizations continue to argue that FTF interaction is more rewarding and satisfying. If anything, the opposite is true. One study compared the decision quality of untrained FTF, brainstorming, and nominal groups. Brainstorming groups and nominal groups were more satisfied, felt their groups used a more effective process, and felt they had communicated more effectively than the untrained FTF groups. Bottom line: the most effective and rewarding creative teams have structure and are not free-for-alls!

As you might imagine, there is some concern that electronic brainstorming might lead to a loss of informal face-to-face communication. And there is indeed reason to be concerned. Teams that abolish all face-to-face meetings run the risk of creating an antagonistic atmosphere. One Silicon Valley company abolished its weekly face-to-face meetings because they were considered to be too bloated—a waste of time. Yet, this ultimately resulted in a toxic workplace. Thus, if the team happens to be colocated, go ahead and set up meetings—but use the structure outlined—rather than just having an anything-goes free-for-all.

In summary, adding some structure to the creative collaboration via the nominal group technique, brainwriting, or cyberstorming can dramatically increase productivity and make the process more rewarding and less frustrating. These are all examples of the hybrid approach to creative collaboration that can supercharge the team.

Benign and Malignant Conflict

I set up a global team assignment in one of my classes. The goal was to give the students a collaborative experience working with people across the world. This was of interest to the students because over 50 percent of them expected to have a significant management challenge abroad. In the exercise, managers from over twelve countries participated in groups of four to five people. The students eagerly jumped into the project. Armed with an array of state-of-the-art technology, each global team tackled the first order of business—to set up a conference call using Skype-type technology. Despite the carefully laid plans, over 50 percent of the scheduled conference calls did not take place as planned! The problem was not a technology failure. Nor was it motivation. Instead, there was a simple communication problem. The students relied on the "world clock" to determine the time of the call, but failed to learn about idiosyncratic differences in countries and time zones not observing daylight savings time! Unfortunately, the students did not realize the source of the problem and instead blamed each other. That day, I received several e-mails from my students complaining about the "lousy work ethic" of the "foreign" students. At the same time I received these e-mails, the coordinating professors in the other host countries were receiving e-mails from their students complaining about the "unreliability of the US students"! The peer evaluations at the end of the semester confirmed that the local team members held the remotely located members responsible for the debacle.

The experience of the students in my class is an example of *relationship conflict*—conflict that is not about the task, but rather, about personalities and underlying intensions. Relationship conflict is personal, emotional, accusatory, and parties often don't trust or respect one another. Worse yet, the longer relationship conflict goes unaddressed, the more likely it will grow and spread. When it spreads, it becomes *malignant conflict*. For example, when the students in my class immediately leaped to assumptions about the lack of goodwill, dedication, and work ethic, and began trading stories among one another and across groups, the conflict became malignant. The subsequent meetings did not go as well, and other team members spoke in harsh terms about what had happened. Rumors about what had occurred even spread to other teams that did not initially have problems. In short, the conflict quickly grew out of control and poisoned the working relationships of team members.

In contrast to relationship conflict is a different type of conflict that is centered on the task at hand and is known as *task conflict*. For example, if someone does not materialize for a scheduled conference call, it could very well be because the person is lazy and unreliable (as suspected by my students), but it could also be that there was another, much more benign explanation, such as the time zone difference (as in the case I've described) or a technology failure. Unlike relationship conflict, which is personal and emotional, task conflict is usually impersonal, task-focused, and contained. For this reason, task conflict is usually benign, in the sense that it does not threaten to damage the relationship between the parties involved or spread to others in the organizational network. A telltale sign of benign conflict is that the protagonists talk about the altercation immediately after it occurs, make adjustments, and then follow through.

Let's consider another example. Suppose that two research scientists, Jerry and Jenny, hold very different theories about light. Now suppose that they are both planning to attend the same annual research convention to present their theories. They see each other in the convention center. When Jerry sees Jenny, he starts calling her names and walks over to her poster board and leaves a nasty comment. The next day, Jenny attends Jerry's presentation, raises her hand, and says, "This guy is really stupid and the theory is nonsense!" Most scientists who have opposing theories would not conduct themselves in this manner. Rather, it would be more usual for Jenny to raise a particularly incisive question during the presentation and put Jerry on the spot by asking him to recall the exact statistical significance of a complex test or perhaps citing another investigation that she feels Jerry might not have read and asking him to explain the differences. Most of us could not imagine the personal attack occurring among highly educated professionals. Yet it occurs in many companies.

For example, Steve Ballmer, former CEO of Microsoft, was known for his over-the-top displays of emotion. In 2005, Mark Lucovsky alleged in a sworn statement to a Washington state court that Ballmer grew enraged upon hearing that Lucovsky intended to leave Microsoft and take a job at Google. He described Ballmer picking up his chair and throwing it across his office. Then came the angry threat: referring to Google CEO Eric Schmidt, Ballmer vowed to "kill Google" in an expletive-laden tirade.

Another example of malignant conflict occurred in 2011 when Wisconsin Supreme Court Justice Ann Walsh Bradley accused fellow justice David Prosser of putting his hands around her neck in a choke hold after a disagreement got heated in Bradley's office. Similarly, a new industry has emerged in medicine, with coaches and consultants providing anger management to curb the temper tantrums thrown by doctors in the surgical room. According to George Anderson, a consultant who offers anger management training for professionals, verbal abuse is among the milder transgressions—throwing surgical instruments such as scalpels is not unusual.

Jeer Pressure

Jeer pressure, a term coined by Leslie Janes and James Olson, occurs when people watch others in their team being ridiculed or taunted. When we watch others poke fun at people, we unconsciously inhibit our own behavior. In short, jeer pressure increases conformist, conventional thinking; when people observed videotapes in which people were either ridiculing others, ridiculing themselves, or not ridiculing anyone, those who heard others being ridiculed were the most conforming and more afraid of failing compared to those who watched self-ridicule or no ridicule.

Conflict Sweet Spot

As you might sense, relationship conflict is generally not productive. Task conflict is often (but not always) productive. However, although too little or too much task conflict can thwart effectiveness, there is a "sweet spot" where moderate amounts of task conflict have beneficial effects. In one investigation, top management teams in 109 US hospitals examined the relationship between the amount of task conflict on the team and the teams' decision quality and found teams with moderate amounts of conflict were the most effective. This section introduces methods to ensure that teams engage in the right amount of conflict.

To Debate or Not to Debate?

There is an apparent contradiction in the advice given to team leaders. On the one hand, teams and leaders are strongly advised by decision scholars to introduce devil's advocates, debate, and critical thinking into group meetings. On the other hand, creativity researchers admonish teams to set aside all evaluation and judgment and banish devil's advocates. Indeed, one of Alex Osborn's cardinal rules of effective brainstorming was to eliminate judgment and evaluation of ideas. Thus, leaders are the victims of a mixed message: *"Don't criticize others, yet engage in dissent!"* Which is correct? As it turns out, debate and competing views have positive value and stimulate divergent, creative ideas. One study investigated traditional brainstorming instructions, debate-and-criticize instructions, and control condition. Debate instructions were superior to traditional brainstorming instructions in at least two cultures—the United States and France. Teams that engage in task conflict are more likely to engage in innovative behavior and knowledge sharing behaviors. Conversely, teams that engage in relationship conflict shared less knowledge.

Saving Face and Losing Face

In our own research, my colleagues and I have found that another factor that mediates the ability to benefit from task conflict is the degree to which people need to save face or protect their own image. Think about the people on your own team. Are some people extremely sensitive? Are some people easily threatened, embarrassed, or worried about their image? People who are particularly thin-skinned might take offense even when they are challenged about a task. Indeed, when people who are highly sensitive are challenged, they react emotionally. Face-saving—the need for people to preserve their image or avoid losing dignity—is at the root of much social embarrassment. Some people have a much higher need than others to feel dignified and respected by others.

My colleagues Judith White, Rene Tynan, and Adam Galinsky and I conducted a series of experiments on how people who are sensitive and thus have high face-saving needs can create problems for mutually beneficial interaction. We first needed to find people who seemed particularly sensitive and also people who were not particularly socially sensitive. To do this, we asked people to respond to three simple statements: "I don't respond well to direct criticism"; "My feelings get hurt easily"; and "I am pretty thin-skinned." We then clustered the data into three groups and found that the thinnest-skinned people were the most likely to storm out of a potentially lucrative, win-win negotiation opportunity. Moreover, in mock job negotiations, candidates with thin skins were less likely to negotiate in effective win-win, creative fashion. People with thin skins are quick to take offense and become competitive instead of collaborative. Maybe you have particularly thin skin or maybe you don't, but someone on your team does.

Find Your Schizophrenic Self

Try this as an exercise: the next time you are in a meeting, have someone count the number of times people say "we," "us," or "ours" and also the number of times people say "I," "me," or "mine." I often do this surreptitiously in a meeting and then after the meeting, have the nerve give everyone a We-to-Me ratio score. People with higher scores are more "we" focused. (In our research on the "we versus me" effect, my colleagues and I had some people read a simple paragraph that focused on family and interconnections (we); we had others read a simple paragraph that focused on independence (me). Then, we examined their subsequent behavior in a completely unrelated situation: a tense, fractious dispute. Those who had read the "we" paragraph were more constructive and less likely to reach an impasse than those who had read the "me" paragraph.

Then, as a follow-up, start listening for your own pronouns and, as I like to say, "find your schizophrenic self." Every time you hear yourself say, "I," "me," or "mine," try to rephrase it using "we," "us," and "ours." Using the language of "we" puts our focus on the collective interests of the group.

Writing on the Wall

In one of my workshops focused on creating win-win negotiation techniques for clients and their companies, I observed a somewhat curious phenomenon. It involved flip charts and whiteboards. In one exercise, several teams of people were challenged with a particularly contentious buyer-seller negotiation. Unbeknownst to negotiators, a creative "A-ha!" best solution was possible, but it was not easy to see. That is, unless protagonists were willing to ask questions, brainstorm, and consider a lot of possibilities. As it happened, we were in a facility in which some people met in rooms that were impoverished in the sense that they did not have any flip charts or whiteboards. Others were negotiating in rooms that were stocked with flip charts and whiteboards. Other than that, there were no discernible differences. The groups who had access to flip charts were not explicitly instructed to use them— but they spontaneously did. And then a curious thing happened— they started writing suggestions and editing various drafts of proposals. Those without flip charts made decidedly fewer proposals and seemed to lose motivation. Most notably, those using the flip charts were the most likely to craft creative, win-win deals. When people put their words on paper, they can attack the paper, rather than attacking the person. This prevents a stare down and creates a single text to which both parties can contribute. Many times confusion arises when people are talking. Writing things down immediately clarifies potential misunderstandings.

When Stuck, Summarize

During conflict, people often become frustrated and stymied because they don't know how to find a way out. Instead of expressing frustration and defeat in such moments, summarize;

for example, "Look, I feel angry too and I worry about things that are going to come out of my mouth. I think we have been in a defensive mode and I would like to see us move toward problem solving."

Separate Accept-Reject Discussions from Rank Ordering

One of my clients asked me when is the right time to tell the other party that something is "not negotiable." I told that client, "Never." Too often, people in conflict will claim that certain courses of action are unacceptable or nonnegotiable. I advise my clients and students to put aside the language of "accept or reject" and instead opt for the language of rank ordering and prioritizing.

What's Your "Tell"?

Most people have a characteristic style of dealing with conflict in their personal and professional lives. I call this your *conflict tell.* Frankly, the way we deal with conflict with a boss is not likely to be dramatically different from how we deal with conflict with a spouse. To begin your self-discovery process, think of a significant conflict you have recently had with someone you care about (i.e., not a one-off conflict with an airline attendant or service manager at a hotel, etc.). Rather, think about a long-term coworker, teammate, or superior. If necessary, think about your spouse! Of the four following behaviors, which would you say best characterizes how you behaved during that conflict?

Avoid: You ignored the conflict; avoided the other person to the extent you were able to do so; wrote the other person off; circumvented a discussion because it seemed fruitless, hopeless, too painful, not worth your time, etc.

Rationalize: You tolerated the relationship; rationalized the other person's behaviors; hoped the situation would resolve itself; tried to be understanding and accepting of the difficult situation; maybe even made excuses for the other person (e.g., "If he was not jetlagged, I'm sure that he would have thanked me for getting the project done on time.").

Attack: You engaged in direct combat; stepped right up and told the other person off; recruited whatever resources were necessary to stand your ground and block or thwart the other person.

Engage: You attempted to initiate a clarifying discussion with the other person; talked about your goals; acknowledged your own faults; separated the past from the future.

These four patterns represent how people often deal with interpersonal conflict. And your signature conflict style at home is often what you bring to work. Thus, if you often retreat from conflict at work or attempt to tune the other person out, you are probably doing this at home as well. The key thing to think about is: what behavior are you reinforcing in the other party? In other words, if you are engaging in avoidance, the other person has no doubt gotten the message that you are unavailable.

Conversely, if you use attack mode, chances are you have created a boxing match with the other party. This is what is meant by an *escalating conflict spiral*.

If you have rationalized the conflict and tried to keep a stiff upper lip, you have not been honest with yourself or the other party. There is never a right time for conflict. Conflict is always inconvenient. But if you don't take care of it, it is going to rear its head in an ugly way.

So, what course of action is best to take? An abundance of evidence suggests that it is only through engagement that conflict can result in productive outcomes. Avoidance, rationalization, or outright attacks are not optimal for solving conflict. People who use avoidance suppress conflict. If you suppress conflict, it often manifests itself in very unpleasant ways, such as poor health, passive-aggressive behavior, and the deterioration of relationships. Those who rationalize conflict are bound to eventually reach their breaking point. By making excuses for the other party, we are not treating them with the respect they ultimately deserve. The problem is that most people don't know how to start productive engagement because they are afraid or quite simply, have given up hope.

One of my favorite interview questions is, "Tell me about a conflict you had with someone at work and what you did to resolve it." If the job candidate answers, "I don't have conflicts with people," then I'm immediately suspicious. If they say that the people with whom they have had conflict with in their organizational career have been psychopaths (and proceed to give me full-blown personality profiles), then they lack self-awareness. If they say that they ignored these people, hoped they would change, or attacked them, I also score them below average. Why? People who are emotionally intelligent realize that conflict is inevitable in the workplace and they deal proactively with conflict (rather than reactively, passively, or aggressively).

The key to successful conflict management begins with self-awareness. If you are unaware that you are feeling angry, misunderstood, unappreciated, or defiant, you will be unable to move forward with proactive conflict management.

Once you have become self-aware, the next step is to inform the team of what is going on. The main principle to keep in mind here is that you need to take ownership of your beef with the team and avoid making the assertion that they have "caused" your problem.

To make this concrete, let's take the case of Lisa, who feels that the team makes an inordinate number of requests and demands of her and does not ask her about how this will affect her workload. In short, Lisa feels unappreciated, not respected, and "dumped on." What should Lisa do?

> Don't say: "I am fed up with how you guys are dumping on me. You don't show me any respect and you don't appreciate all that I do and I'm at the end of my rope and I won't take it anymore."

> Do say: "I feel frustrated and unappreciated when I get requests to do work that is in addition to what we have previously discussed. I want to discuss how to make things work better."

Engagement

Let's suppose you have decided to not avoid conflict and not rationalize it away. You feel like attacking, but instead you have committed yourself to having a real conversation. How do you begin? The phrase "Talk to Joe productively about our conflict" is not in anyone's Outlook calendar!

You don't want to ambush the other party. Instead, you need a *lead-in* to initiate engagement. Some of my favorite lead-ins, which have been pilot-tested by plenty of my clients and students, are:

- Harry, I would like to have a level two conversation about the project and check signals. What is a good time? I will work around your schedule.

- Susan, I feel uncomfortable talking about the project, but I'm unhappy with the current situation and suspect you might feel the same way. I'm hoping we can work out a time to check signals.

- Chris, I need to talk to you about something that is bothering me. I want to try to work this out before I start feeling resentful.

Once you have led into the conversation and carved out a time to talk, make sure you speak to this person, keeping to the following guidelines:

- Use verbs, forget the adjectives: Adjectives get us into trouble. It is much better to use verbs or behavioral descriptions. For example, compare phrases like "You are controlling" and "You are judgmental" (adjectives) with "I was upset when you did not consult me" and "I was taken aback when you criticized me in the meeting last Thursday," which reference an action or behavior. So, be descriptive via referencing behaviors and actions rather than evaluative. By focusing on behaviors and actions rather than internal states, the receiver of feedback is able to better change their behavior. Consider the difference between, "You seem lazy and uninvolved at work" versus "You arrive fifteen minutes late and you don't ask for others' help in projects." The former is blaming and immediately puts the other person on the defensive. The second is fact-based.

- Be specific, not general: Do not use the terms, "You always . . ." or "You never . . ." but rather, "Sometimes . . ." or preferably, "Last Wednesday . . ."

- Speak for yourself: We often show our anger and resentment by forming coalitions against someone. For example, consider a colleague who approaches a business associate and says, "You know, several people were talking about how we don't like how you are allocating the budget . . ." It is important to speak only for yourself. Otherwise, the person might become so defensive that he or she will be unable to hear the substance of your message. Do not say, "Everybody thinks . . ." or "Everybody feels the same way I do." Instead, speak for yourself.

- Ideally, find something positive to say: People don't get enough positive feedback. So find something you actually do admire about this person—or something she does better than others—and compliment her.

- Express optimism about change: It is very important to emphasize that you not only care about the other person, but you believe that he has the power and ability to change and develop. Carol Dweck cites the belief in one's own ability to adapt and learn as the single most important key to success. For this reason, people who believe their skills are innately determined are less resilient than people who believe their skills are malleable.

Your Brain on Feedback

Most people say they want to hear the truth about how they are perceived, but in fact, it is often so frightening to get feedback that we don't react in a way that allows us to benefit. We often go into a flight-or-fight mode.

I get more questions about *giving* feedback than almost any other topic. What is interesting, however, is that I get very few questions about *receiving* feedback. One of the first principles I teach my students is that to be entitled to offer feedback to someone, you must be open to receiving feedback. The first principle when someone offers you feedback is to *thank them*. Think of it this way: someone cares enough or thinks you are important enough to bother to do something about. So, express gratitude when someone offers you feedback. Feedback is a gift, so say thank you or, even better, send a note or card.

The second principle is to be open to feedback. Don't ask, "How am I doing?"; ask "What can I work on?" Signal openness to feedback. However, just because you might see yourself as a person who can accept feedback, it in no sense guarantees that you are signaling that you are open to receiving feedback. And if you are hoping that your casual remark to your staff and subordinates that they should let you know if they have any feedback will get them to really speak their minds—well, just forget that. Rather, the burden is squarely on you to set the appropriate stage to receive feedback.

For example, Leo Babauta asked his readers for feedback to improve his blog, *Zen Habits*. After receiving a heavy dose of critical feedback, he returned all e-mails and thanked the readers for their comments. Similarly, Ken Mills, CEO of creative media company Mills James, solicited direct feedback from his employees when the company began expanding. He instituted a series of nonmanagerial employee meetings where feedback (and criticism) could be leveled without fear of reprisal. He admits that criticism of a personal nature, though sometimes necessary, can be a tough pill to swallow. "Sometimes I get depressed after these meetings. But I think the main thing is, that even more than what you do, is that the people feel like they are being heard. That goes a long way."

Here are three guidelines that will help you process feedback:

- Ask for examples: Remember that the people offering you feedback may not follow the guidelines of constructive (informational) feedback. That's okay. So, if they are using evaluative language, then don't lecture them about the importance of using behavioral examples, just ask them to give you examples. If they can't come up with any, then refer to meetings in the recent past and ask for them to give feedback pertaining to that situation or meeting.

- Separate agreement from understanding: Just because a person is offering you feedback does not mean you need to agree with it. It also does not mean you need to argue with this person. Rather, you can probe for understanding and set aside the question of whether you agree or not. I will warn you that this is hard to do, but think about these sentence stems, "I'm not sure I can agree with that or not, at least until I get some more examples of the controlling behavior you are referring to. Can we talk about whether you saw such behavior in the new program launch?" or perhaps, "I'm not sure I see it the same way you do, but can you give me some more examples that I can think about?"

- Focus on the future; do not attempt to justify the past: Most of the time, people become very defensive about the criticism that others offer them. Thus, they tend to dig up the past, explain and justify and rationalize their behavior, which really serves no purpose. However, it is a far more effective use of everybody's time to focus on what can be done in the future so as not to repeat past missteps.

Trust and Respect

People on teams need to care and to trust each other. Trust and respect are both important for teams, but they are not the same thing. *Trust* is the willingness of a person to rely on another person in the absence of monitoring or supervision. Conversely, *respect* is the level of esteem a person has for another.

To measure the amount of *trust* you have in your team, how much do you agree with the following statements?

1. I trust my teammates.

2. I have little faith that my teammates will consider my needs when making decisions.

3. I believe that my teammates are truthful and honest.

If you answered yes to items 1 and 3, but no to item 2, then you have high trust in your team.

To assess the amount of *respect* for your team, indicate how much you agree or disagree with these statements:

1. I think highly of my teammates' character.

2. This team sets a good example.

3. Our team does things the right way.

4. My team deserves my consideration.

5. I admire my teammates.

6. I am proud to be part of my team.

7. I think my teammates have useful perspectives.

8. My teammates usually have good reasons for their beliefs.

9. People on my team have well-founded ideas.

10. I hold my team in high regard.

11. I think highly of my team members.

12. Our team has reason to be proud.

13. I respect my teammates.

If you answered the majority of these questions with "true" or "I highly agree," that is a good indication that you have respect for your teammates. If you answered the majority of questions with "false" or "I disagree," that is an indication that respect is lacking.

Here's another way to think of the difference between trust and respect: suppose your colleague has failed his pilot's license test three times because he has an uncorrectable vision problem. However, he is a wonderful, generous person who is very smart. Most rational people would never get in a plane with him if he were to fly it because he lacks competence. We trust his intentions, but we don't respect his competence. We are (wisely) unwilling to make ourselves vulnerable when we don't respect someone's competence. Now, imagine you have another colleague who is an expert, decorated pilot, but knows that you have queasy stomach. You have occasionally wondered whether this person wishes to intimidate you or make you sick to your stomach. You would most likely not board her plane—not because of a competence issue, but because you don't trust her intentions. The first example is a respect issue; the second example is a trust issue. Ideally, we need both trust and respect in our teams. Teams high in respect but low in trust often appear as collections of individualists, afraid of exposing their vulnerabilities for fear they might be exploited. Conversely, teams high in trust but low in respect are safe but ineffective because they don't see much value in the contributions of their teammates, even if they are well intentioned.

People need to recognize the expertise of others (respect others' competence) and also trust their intentions. Trust is the willingness to make yourself vulnerable to achieve a greater goal.

People in teams size up how "safe" they feel in bringing up certain subjects and seeking assistance from their team. *Psychological safety* is the extent to which people feel that they can raise issues and questions without fear of being criticized, scorned, or rebuffed.

What does it take to develop the collaborative spirit in people? Trust is critical for effective collaboration. Trust occurs when people are willing to be *vulnerable* in their relationships with others.

Many people have a difficult time being vulnerable with their teams. When we depend on others, we need to trust their skill and we need to trust their intentions. That is the only way we really learn. However, just like the airplane pilot example, we need to be judicious about whom we put our trust in.

There appears to be at least one caveat to the trust-is-good-for-creativity mandate. In one investigation, people were either exposed to subliminal distrust messages—below the threshold of their conscious awareness or subliminal trust messages—again, below the threshold of their awareness. If you ask these folks, they will tell you they were not aware of seeing anything. However, their brain took in the subliminal message and this led to an interesting twist: those who had been exposed to the subliminal distrust message were more likely to display cognitive flexibility— the opposite of rigid thinking! Why? Distrust provokes people to think about nonobvious alternatives to potentially deceptive appearances. Thus, even though people were not even consciously aware that they had been subliminally exposed to distrust, their brains started to spontaneously solve a problem by thinking outside of the boundaries!

⚓ Chapter Capstone

When managed well, conflict enhances team performance. The problem is that most people are afraid of conflict. Part of this fear is rooted in the fact that they have seen the damage that can result from open attack and jeering. However, there is a healthier type of conflict that is problem- rather than people-focused. Leaders need to be role models for effective conflict expression and also need to know how to move away from an attack. Leaders also need to know how to use the group's scarcest resource—time—and so this chapter also touched on how to neutralize overly dominant people. If there is a conflict sweet spot, it is engagement that involves being specific, using verbs, and expressing optimism about change.

CHAPTER 7

Setting the Stage for a Creative Conspiracy

Suppose that you had a large budget to organize a creative retreat for your company. Your objective is to set the stage for the open flow of ideas and explore possibilities for an important new initiative. Consider two companies—X and Y—who were in such a position. Company X decided upon a five-star, world-class resort with spectacular golfing and luxurious spa facilities. Upon checking in, team members received a lavish gift bag containing rare wine, 800-gram Turkish cotton beach towels, and more. They dined in stately rooms with private chefs and lingered for hours over gourmet meals. Their brainstorming sessions took place in twenty-five-hundred-square-foot palatial rooms with mirrored walls, vaulted ceilings, and imported chandeliers. A personal massage therapist was hired as well. Company Y chose a small, boutique hotel located in a trendy, urban city. The team worked in a small meeting room—about five hundred square feet—and they removed the chairs and stocked it with moveable sitting cubes. One of the walls was covered with whiteboard, one with cork and thumbtacks, another with flip charts, and one was a smart LCD screen that could project laptop and video images. Each day, lunches arrived from different local ethnic restaurants and a tasting was set up on a picnic blanket spread on a table that was moved in and out of the room. A trained meeting facilitator was hired. Upon leaving the retreat week, company X members reported feeling refreshed, relaxed, and ready to ease back into the stresses of work. Company Y members made huge strides on a new product concept.

In our work with companies and teams, my colleagues and I see many more examples of company X meetings than company Y meetings. Hotels and resorts are not experts in the creative process—they are experts in the relaxation process. We have to remember this when we orchestrate the working conditions to set the stage for creative collaboration. In this chapter, I introduce best practices for instigating a creative conspiracy in your team—whether you are at an off-site or right at the office. When done right, the creative stage gives teams permission to act in a very different way that most people find liberating and productive.

This chapter gives leaders practical tools on how to best structure meetings so they are productive, vibrant, and fun, whether the meeting is fifteen minutes long or a weekend off-site. The following best practices are all scientifically based and, with all due respect to consultants, none should cost more than $5 or so (mostly for materials that can be purchased in a dime store).

Brainstorming 1.0

I use the term Brainstorming 1.0 to refer to the original rules of brainstorming that are still common practice today. Most businesses owe an enormous debt to a man they've never met or even heard of. That man is Alex Osborn, and he was the person who coined the term *brainstorming*. Osborn was not a stuffy academic, holed up in an ivory tower. Alex Osborn worked for a living in an advertising company and even more important, he believed in the power of the team. Osborn quite simply believed that the whole creative team could be much greater than the sum of its parts if they followed four simple rules, which he put forth in his book *Applied Imagination*. The reason Osborn has been so influential is that the rules were simple, memorable, made sense, and were nearly costless to institute and to a great extent, they *worked*.

1. Expressiveness

First, Osborn argued that members of creative groups should freely and unabashedly express any idea that came to mind, however fanciful or strange; members should not hold back or censor any ideas.

2. No Criticism

Osborn wisely realized that expressiveness would be possible only if members did not criticize one another. So, Osborn's second rule was to set aside all judgment, blame, and any discussion of "We've tried that before" or "It's too expensive" or "We'll never sell that to upper management."

3. Quantity

Osborn wisely noted that if the team's goal is high quality, people will choke or freeze up because it is simply not possible to will ourselves to generate breakthrough ideas on demand. So, Osborn set aside quality and simply urged the group to generate lots of ideas, knowing that quantity might paradoxically lead to quality.

I have realized the same thing in my own research. If I tell a young PhD student who is developing a dissertation thesis to develop a paradigm-shifting idea, that student will surely jump out of the nearest window. However, if I tell him to think of three to four ideas that might have already been proposed, might be untestable, boring, or even politically incorrect, he can certainly do that.

I had my own wake-up call in 1995, when I was on sabbatical at the Center for Advanced Study in Palo Alto. The next-door scholar-in-residence was Gary Alan Fine, the prolific sociologist. It was June, and I had only managed to write two chapters of my first book. Meanwhile Gary was working on no fewer than four books and had had a prolific year of writing. I was dejected. One day Gary invited me into his writing cabin—a virtual cave of creativity. On the walls were hastily scrawled notes, and piles of papers covered the floor. The office looked somewhat like a scene from *A Beautiful Mind*, when John Nash (played by Russell Crowe) had holed himself up in a garage, convinced that he was at the center of a communist conspiracy. Gary then walked me over to one of the walls and explained how many pages he had written for each of his four in-progress books that day. It was clear that quantity was what he cared about. Then he looked at me and said, "At the end of a day, I've got something I can edit. It does not matter if it is good or bad. What matters is that something is on a page." After that day in his office, I set aside my impossibly high standards and just started to put my ideas on the page, following Gary's advice. I learned to go through many drafts and became a writer. I finished my first book in the next month, and in the next year, I wrote another. Whenever I feel stuck, I think back to that day in Gary's office and his advice to just put something on paper.

Building

Of all of his wise rules, Osborn's principle of *synergy* best captured his deeply held belief in the power of the creative team. According to Osborn, because all of the ideas belong to the team, anyone should feel free to modify, extend, connect, and otherwise build on the ideas of others. The concept of *building* involves combining ideas. It's the truly synergistic aspect of groups. The synergistic combination of ideas is what is meant when we say the whole can be greater than the sum of the parts.

Paul Paulus's research team undertook an analysis of the building concept in brainstorming. People were presented with either a list of rare or common ideas to combine and build on. They did this as either individuals or groups. Sure enough, groups generated fewer combinations (builds) than did nominal groups. However, the groups were more creative when combining rare ideas. The message? Groups benefit best from building on rare ideas.

In my courses, I often refer to Osborn's original four rules as *first-generation brainstorming* or *brainstorming 1.0*. They are worth their weight in gold—they have improved the performance of creative teams perhaps more than any other practical prescription. At the most basic level, they are effective because they are *rules*—and there is plenty of evidence that groups that have rules outperform groups that do not have rules, even if the rules are not ideal. Over and above that, these four rules are particularly valuable in their own right. Indeed, the scientific evidence strongly indicates that groups who use these four rules are more creative than groups who don't.

Of all the rules, it is the quantity goal that is the most important. Brainstorming rules alone do not convey a distinct advantage over even a vague quantity goal (presented alone) in terms of enhancing fluency. However, brainstorming rules are definitely useful adjuncts to specific, difficult quantity goals.

The practice of brainstorming is so ingrained in most organizations today that most people claim to know the cardinal rules of brainstorming by heart. Most people believe that it is important to suggest wild ideas, encourage others, and have no rules. However, only about 50 percent of this advice is backed up by research. To make matters worse, what people believe brainstorming is and what they actually do are noticeably different.

What I see most often in company brainstorming meetings is a flagrant violation of the cardinal rules of brainstorming. Brainstorming sessions often fail to separate idea generation from idea evaluation, and a few people usually dominate the discussion. I've also witnessed a well-intentioned group leader charging the group to think of ideas that are "very new and very useful." That leader has just planted the seeds for self-censoring and a fruitless meeting, with people too petrified to speak up.

Brainstorming 6.0

In this section, I introduce some additional rules to Osborn's original four tenets. Think of these new guidelines as supplements to the original four—not replacements. Just as when a software developer releases an improved operating system or utility, creativity scholars have continued to improve and perfect upon the original rules. Thus, I refer to these improvements and refinements as Brainstorming 6.0. Over fifty years have passed since Osborn's book was published, and his cardinal rules have withstood the test of time. Nevertheless, Paul Paulus, professor at University of Texas at Arlington and author of *Group Creativity: Innovation Through Collaboration*, wondered whether there might be some additional, highly practical rules that companies and teams could adopt that would supplement Osborn's original four. After observing that people in teams often are verbose and drift off topic, Paulus and his colleagues designed a clever experiment to test the efficacy of four new brainstorming rules. They coached some groups to follow Osborn's original rules and other groups to follow not only Osborn's rules, but also the four new rules:

1. Stay focused on the task.

2. Don't tell stories or explain ideas.

3. When no one is suggesting an idea, restate the problem and encourage ideas.

4. Encourage those people who are not talking to make a contribution.

The results of the study were powerful and straightforward; the new rules generated a huge return on investment. Groups that followed the additional rules generated nearly 50 percent more ideas (quantity increase). Groups that followed the 6.0 rules also generated a greater number of unique ideas. One of the most profound changes that happened in the new-rules groups was that they used their time more efficiently. They expressed ideas in about sixty words, while groups using the traditional brainstorming rules generally used over 120 words to express an idea! Most people who have stomached a long, bloated company meeting can appreciate parsimony.

Have a Facilitator Enforce the Rules and Run the Meeting

Facilitators have a huge effect on the productivity of face-to-face (FTF) brainstorming groups. Groups with a facilitator outperform groups that do not have a facilitator. And face-to-face groups generate as many ideas as nominal groups when they are assisted by a trained facilitator.

When choosing a facilitator, it is important to have someone who is regarded as unbiased and trustworthy. It is best if the facilitator focuses purely on process and resists inserting substantive ideas. The facilitator should make it clear what the working rules of the meeting are and, ideally, demonstrate what constitutes a rule violation. Most important, the facilitator must be a good umpire; this means that the facilitator won't be popular and liked by everyone, but must call them as he or she sees them.

Set a Clear Goal

It is important to set aside discussions of quality, value, and acceptability in a pure brainstorming meeting and instead, focus purely on volume. Quality is elusive; quantity is attainable. And, the data speak for themselves. Groups that are given a realistic, stretch goal of quantity outperform those that are not given a quantity or quality goal. Paul Paulus's team compared four types of groups: groups that had no goal/focus, groups that had a quantity goal, groups that had a quality goal, and those that aimed for both quantity and quality. Those given the quantity goal performed dramatically better than the other three types of groups!

Left to their own devices, real groups don't seem to set quantity goals. But when they do, they are much more effective. And, if their goals are based on what a nominal group actually achieved, the productivity gap narrows. Indeed, the productivity gap that usually exists between interactive groups and nominal groups can be eliminated by giving interactive groups a performance standard comparable to that attained by a typical nominal group. When the goal is perceived as extremely challenging, creativity is enhanced.

Thus, quantity goals improve the performance of groups. But what about the goal of generating unusual ideas? The goal of generating novel solutions also improves group performance. In one investigation, the performance of groups following Osborn's rules of brainstorming was compared with that of groups that were given the task of coming up with *novelty goals*—unusual or unique ideas that are unlikely to be mentioned by others. In this field experiment, specific novelty goals, whether presented alone or in conjunction with brainstorming rules, improved creative performance. The practicality and effectiveness of participants' ideas were measured by blind coders—who were unbiased in terms of evaluating ideas. Novelty goals did not simply improve the quantity of ideas generated; in fact, the novelty goals improved creative idea generation.

Train People in Idea-Generation Skills

Because most people have not been trained in brainstorming, the mere experience of being in a brainstorming group does not in any way guarantee that they will engage in best practices. When done right, a brainstorming meeting is very different than a regular meeting, and it should feel different. For this reason, I am careful to coach leaders to change gears and bring in very specific tools when the goal is brainstorming, as opposed to problem solving or crisis management. One study trained people in idea generation skills and then compared the creativity of groups specifically trained in idea generation skills with those who had simply been given an equivalent amount of practice (without formal training). Training had a significant, positive effect on creative fluency and originality. The groups who had been trained in idea generation brainstormed more ideas and more original ideas than did groups who simply practiced without training.

Another investigation examined the impact of experiential training on creativity. Specifically, the productivity of groups who engaged in an experiential learning training program was compared to groups who did not have experiential learning and groups who simply brainstormed. The groups who learned brainstorming through experiential learning had significantly higher quantity and quality scores and they also implemented more of their ideas.

One way of encouraging idea-generation skills is through the use of word association. Hamit Coşkun, a professor at Abant Izzet Baysal University in Turkey, examined how word associations that are closely related (such as apple/pear) might actually stimulate greater creativity than remote associations (such as apple/fish). Two groups of people both did a ten-minute word-association warm-up immediately before a brainstorming session. One group warmed up by free-associating to closely paired words; the other group warmed up by free-associating to distantly paired words. The group that warmed up using the close associations generated more ideas, more categories, and deeper ideas than did the groups that were given the remote associations.

All in all, it makes sense for leaders and their teams to take the time to learn the unique rules of idea generation. Do not assume this is obvious. If necessary, spend a day or half a day training one group, tape the training, and then use that as a training device for future groups. I find the best way to teach a new behavior is to show it in action.

Train People in Idea-Selection Skills

Brainstorming (ideation) is one thing. But, what about choosing ideas from a list of brainstormed ideas? Sounds easy, right? Hardly. For most people, idea selection is not significantly better than chance! Most people tend to select ideas that are feasible and desirable, at the expense of originality. Not surprisingly, when people are explicitly instructed to select creative and original ideas, they are better at choosing and selecting the best ideas.

Some might argue that interactive groups might have an edge when it comes to idea selection. However, there is absolutely *no* scientific evidence that interactive groups are better at selecting ideas as compared with nominal groups. In fact, if anything, nominal groups are more likely to select original ideas. In another investigation, nominal groups generated more ideas and more original ideas than interactive groups but there were no differences in terms of idea selection.

Some people in organizations may reject creative ideas, even when they have personally encouraged their team to be creative! According to researcher Jennifer Mueller and colleagues, people can hold a bias against creativity that is not necessarily overt and can be unconsciously activated when people try to reduce uncertainty. Indeed, when people feel uncertain, they often favor practicality instead of creativity when attempting to recognize a creative idea.

Use a Hybrid Structure

When presented with the (depressing) research that indicates that individuals are superior to teams when it comes to creativity, many people conclude that teams should be dismantled. I politely disagree. Rather, I strongly advocate using a hybrid structure for the creative team process. A hybrid structure combines different modes in a particular sequence that I'll discuss here: alone-then-group, rotating membership, meet-the-new-kid, and multiple subgroups.

Alone-Then-Group

Is it best for people to work first in a group and then individually or vice versa? The data are clear on that point: it is best for people to first work independently (doing brainwriting, for example) and then work together in a group. In fact, people who first brainstorm alone and then move to a group are more creative than those who first work in a group and then independently. Similarly, solitary idea generation prior to group brainstorming is better than group brainstorming followed by solitary idea generation. Thus, a winning hybrid structure is the alone-then-group model. Indeed, groups organized with the alone-then-group hybrid structure generate more ideas, better ideas, and are better able to discern the quality of ideas they generate.

In one set of intriguing experiments, University of Pennsylvania students were divided into groups of four to brainstorm new product concepts for a sports and fitness manufacturer and a home-products manufacturer. The teams were given thirty minutes to brainstorm using a traditional (group only) process. Then, teams were instructed in a hybrid process that involved two distinct phases: ten minutes generating and ranking ideas individually, then twenty minutes discussing the ideas in a group. Their ideas were then evaluated by three separate blind panels. The results? The average quality of the ideas generated by the hybrid process were better than those that came from the traditional process by the equivalent of roughly 30 percentage points. The hybrid process generated three times more ideas than the traditional method in the same amount of time. In addition, the quality rating was higher for the top five ideas produced through the hybrid process.

One word of caution: when adopting an alone-then-group hybrid procedure, warn group members against exchanging ideas with one another during the group phase. Doing so reduces the categories of ideas that are explored in the group. This dampening effect is known as *fixation*, in which people tend to conform to ideas suggested. If this does happen, don't fear, taking a break can stop the decline!

Rotating Membership

During one of our courses, a manager asked us whether company reorganizations help or hinder group creativity. The truth is, we didn't know, because to our knowledge that research study had not been conducted. So my colleague, Hoon-Seok Choi of

Sungkyunkwan University, and I devised a pretty simple simulation: we examined whether groups that stayed intact (i.e., did not experience membership change) would be more creative than groups with "open" boundaries (i.e., experienced membership change). We hypothesized that membership change would stimulate the permanent group members to think of new ideas. In short, we thought that the presence of newcomers might actually stir up original members' old ideas or at least motivate these members to revisit old ideas in new ways. We systematically compared brainstorming teams that stayed intact to brainstorming teams that experienced at least one membership change. Otherwise, everything else remained the same. We found strong evidence that the groups that underwent membership change generated a greater volume of ideas and more flexible ideas than did groups that stayed intact. To be specific, there was a 22 percent increase in the total volume of ideas and a 31 percent increase in the number of different kinds of ideas.

One interpretation of these findings is that people who are new to a group are on their best behavior—perhaps in an effort to gain the respect of the group. Another interpretation is that simply the presence of newcomers facilitates new idea generation. To attempt to tease out which of these explanations was really the causal factor, we conducted a further investigation that examined how the presence of "old-timers" was affected by newcomers. If it was indeed the case that increases in creativity were driven by newcomers, then we should not see any increase in the creativity of old-timers. However, if newcomers spark new ideas in old-timers, we should see increased creativity among these folks. Indeed, that is exactly what we saw. When we taped the brainstorming sessions and removed the contributions made by the newcomers themselves, we saw that the old-timers experienced a surge in creativity. Specifically, there was a 94 percent increase in the number of ideas suggested by the permanent members when a newcomer entered the group (as compared with groups that stayed intact)! And there was a 68 percent increase in the cognitive flexibility of the permanent members. This study provides hard empirical evidence for the adage that new blood stimulates creativity!

The New Kid on the Block

Intact teams, like long-married couples who can complete each other's sentences, often get set in their ways. As they work together, teams develop mental models that guide how they solve problems. Unfortunately, team mental models developed through repeat collaboration may interfere with processes that produce *creative abrasion*. Creative abrasion is the process whereby idea generation occurs because of the group's composition of different people and personalities—because these people actually spur one another to generate new and unique ideas. Recall the advice in chapter 3 to make groups more heterogeneous. The development of the Apple Macintosh computer provides an example. Steve Jobs put together a team of engineers who were also qualified in disparate fields such as art, music, and philosophy. The diversity of the team and the varying thoughts that each individual brought to the team helped to create an atmosphere that did not always bring harmony, but helped to inspire a machine that would soon be in almost everyone's home. Cirque du Soleil CEO Daniel Lamarre believes that traditional brainstorming sessions are ineffective, and insists that a certain degree of tension and creative friction leads to innovation breakthroughs. Accordingly, Cirque du Soleil hires people in their early twenties who have opposing viewpoints, and provocative disagreement is both tolerated and cultivated. Another way to view this concept is to think of the adage "opposites attract." Many times we may look at a group of people and think they would never work well together but they end up making beautiful music together. Such creative abrasion can be stimulated with rotating team membership or the introduction of a temporary visitor.

Competition is another way to spark creativity. In a study of the performance of seventy four-person groups in an idea-generation task, Markus Baer of Washington University examined how competition with other groups affected the creativity exhibited by "open" groups (i.e., those that experienced membership change) and "closed" groups (i.e., those that did not experience membership change). Competition with other, outside groups showed a

U-shaped pattern in open groups (with creativity greatest with low and high levels of competition), but the pattern was distinctly different for the closed groups. For closed groups, only low competition (with outsiders) increased creativity. The implications for creative collaboration are that it is key is to consider both the composition of the group (open or closed) and the level of perceived competition with outside groups: if the group is closed, then competition should be minimized. However, if the group is open, competition can be heightened.

Multiple Subgroups

Another way that a hybrid structure may be created is with the use of multiple subgroups within a larger group. For example, a larger, clumsy team of twenty-five people might create four or five subgroups to work on a given problem. Once this structure has been decided on, the question is whether each group should complete the entire process from start to finish and combine their results at the end (parallel mode) or have each group build on the work provided by previous subgroups (serial mode). The choice depends on whether you want to maximize the variety of new ideas (flexibility) or elaborate and expand upon particular ideas. Groups using serial mode produce more elaborations than parallel groups, but parallel groups produce a greater number of unique ideas than serial groups.

Act Like a Child

There would be no problem with creativity if people simply would not grow up. In one investigation, people were asked to write about what they would do if they had a day off from school now or as their seven-year-old selves. The first group recorded mundane activities, such as catching up on sleep, getting some work done, etc. However, the second group listed things such as buying the biggest lollipop they could find or spend the day playing with friends. The group that wrote about their seven-year-old self performed better on a test of creativity.

Even thinking about being old can affect our behaviors in unconscious ways, through a mental process called *priming*. Indeed, John Bargh of New York University flashed pictures of older people on a computer screen at such a high rate of speed that they were not detectable—consciously, that is. However, unconsciously, the image of the old person triggered a chemical reaction in the brain that resulted in people walking significantly more slowly down a corridor. Apparently, the mere idea of age and aging not only triggers subconscious images and thoughts of slowing down, it affects behavior as well.

Debate Rules

Osborn's cardinal rules of brainstorming admonished people to not criticize their own and others' ideas. This seems like pretty straightforward advice. Yet, when we think about the problems that can result when groups avoid conflict and agree too readily with one another, the advice about setting aside judgment may breed another pernicious group problem—groupthink or excessive like-mindedness. In chapter 6, I recounted Jerry Harvey's tale of the fateful trip to Abilene. If only the family members had spoken up and argued the drawbacks of traveling down the dusty highway, they might have prevented such a senseless waste of a day. The 1961 Bay of Pigs fiasco is a textbook classic for every student of groupthink. Several members of John F. Kennedy's cabinet harbored serious doubts about the far-fetched plan, yet dared not speak up in the presence of their charismatic leader. Dissent, debate, and competing views can ward off excessive like-mindedness in a group, groupthink, and a number of other problems.

World-renowned creativity and brainstorming expert Charlan Nemeth of the University of California, Berkeley, decided to put Osborn's "no evaluation" prescription to the test. In a carefully designed series of studies, Nemeth compared groups who challenged and criticized each other with those who didn't. Thus, some groups were told to debate and even openly criticize one another, and others were advised to not criticize each other. Overall, there was value in both kinds of instructions—as compared with simply not giving *any* instructions! However, in general, groups that debated and criticized each other outperformed the groups that followed the guidance to not criticize and judge one another. In other words, granting teams permission to criticize and debate resulted in higher creativity than traditional brainstorming instructions.

However, there is an important caveat involving the *type* of criticism team members level at one another. Creativity is higher when group members give negative evaluations of *ideas*, but not negative evaluations of the *source* of ideas. Consider for example, the difference in the following two statements: "Hey, Joe, I don't see how it will work to put an electronic shifter on the bike" versus, "Joe does not know what he is talking about." When people criticize ideas but not sources, groups are more creative than when they withhold all evaluation. Moreover, group members are more satisfied when working under conditions of idea-targeted negative evaluations rather than source-targeted or no evaluation. The message for creative collaboration is to be critical of ideas, but respectful of the people.

Don't Get Mad, Get Snarky

It is important to think about your style of criticizing ideas. If you are going to be negative, it is better to be *sarcastic* rather than simply angry. In one field study simulating customer calls to service centers, customers were either angry (e.g., "Your service is extremely inefficient!") or sarcastic (e.g., "Your service is fast as a turtle! You make deliveries only between 9 a.m. and 12 p.m. These hours are just *perfect* for working people!"). The service people were then asked to solve a series of problems. Those who were the targets of anger were better at analytical problem solving, but worse at creative problem solving. Conversely, the targets of sarcasm were better at solving creative problems because the sarcasm stimulated complex thinking and attenuated the otherwise negative effects of anger.

Break the Problem Down

Sometimes, brainstorming tasks can be quite overwhelming, so it's important to break the problem down into manageable parts. Groups can more easily tackle a problem broken down into more bite-size pieces. In one investigation, people were either presented with a simultaneous display of problems at their school (e.g., classes, parking, campus activities) and told to brainstorm about how to improve on them, or they were given a sequential display of the same school problems three minutes apart. The students who were given the sequential display of problems came up with twenty ideas and the students who were given all the problems at once only came up with ten ideas over a thirty-minute period. The implications for creative collaboration are clear: most organizations often face what appear to be monumental challenges—e.g., regaining market share, cutting costs, etc. These problems can be overwhelming unless they are broken down into manageable subparts to attack.

Cognitively Stimulate the Group

One big challenge with brainstorming is that groups quickly run out of steam. For example, one study examined several innovation projects following the actual processes of professional designers. The frequency of idea production (fluency) remained roughly constant during the first thirty minutes, but then steadily declined after this period. More disconcertingly, the number of appropriate (feasible) ideas decreased rapidly, such that 75 percent of the appropriate ideas emerged in the first fifteen of the thirty total minutes. Thus, groups quickly become depleted.

The solution to the depletion problem is to stimulate the group. By *stimulation*, I mean introducing words, pictures, suggestions, different postures, and so on to a group. Such stimulation maintains and, in many cases, increases the frequency of idea generation. Moreover, the stimuli also helps generate more appropriate ideas. Singer Jack White designed his recording studio and office space, Third Man Records, entirely from scratch in order to stimulate his own sense of creativity. The décor reflects his quirky junk-art aesthetic: African masks and shrunken heads from New Guinea; antique phone booths and vintage Victrolas. Inside, the walls that face west are all painted red, and the ones that face east are all painted blue. The exterior, meanwhile, is yellow and black (with a touch of red) with a Tesla tower sitting on the roof. The inside holds secret passageways as well as mounted heads of bison, a giraffe, and a Himalayan tahr. All these trappings help create a unique surrounding and mind space for White and his band members.

Groups that are cognitively stimulated are more creative than those left to their own devices. There are many ways to cognitively stimulate groups. For example, in one investigation, people who were exposed to ideas on audiotape as they were brainstorming generated more ideas. Exchanging ideas with fellow group members does not appear to be as helpful in increasing creativity. In fact, groups given an opportunity to exchange ideas are no more creative than groups not allowed to exchange ideas.

Exposing people to stimulus ideas that are *diverse* (as opposed to homogeneous) improves creativity. Providing examples of possible solutions to problems also enhances creativity. For example, Christina Shalley of the Georgia Institute of Technology conducted a study in which groups were challenged to find solutions to management problems. They were given either a creative example of a solution, a standard (traditional) example, or no example. The creative example was the most effective: people had higher creativity and intrinsic motivation when given a creative example. Those not given an example were the least creative.

A study by Hamit Coşkun examined the effectiveness of two different exercises: divergent (generating many words on *differences* for given dual words) and convergent (generating many words on *similarities* for given dual words). For example, suppose you are given the pair butter/cheese. You would either be asked to generate differences between these words or similarities. People who first did the convergent (similarity) followed by divergent (differences) exercise were more creative than those who did the exercise in reverse, but only when they had first done a divergent thinking exercise. Similarly, divergent thinking with closely linked word associations produced the highest brainstorming performance as compared with convergent thinking style and distant associations. The takeaway is that groups should warm up or practice doing divergent exercises, and then attempt to find similarities, if they want to pump up their creativity.

Deep Exploration

Deep exploration is a particular priming process in which people dig deep down into a category; this is in contrast to a random process in which ideas just come to mind randomly. People in one study went into deep exploration when they were given subcategories of a brainstorming topic prior to a brainstorming session. Priming improves both productivity and originality on the category.

It is important for team leaders to not be limited when it comes to cognitively stimulating the group. It is not necessary to have access to fancy computers, videos, or graphics. Bill Maddux and his colleagues devised a clever technique for people to simply use their own memories as a type of cognitive stimulation. In their investigation, people were asked to recall a multicultural learning experience. Presumably, people who have lived abroad have developed more memories and experiences than people who have only traveled abroad. Indeed, those who have lived abroad were able to creatively leverage their cultural experiences—they were more creative when they recalled their multicultural experiences compared to those who had not lived abroad. Thus, priming or activating these memories enhances creativity on insight, association, and generation tasks.

Start the Clock

Most teams work to fill their time. Even more disconcerting, research indicates that left to their own devices, teams will use whatever time is allotted to them, without appreciable differences in performance! One investigation compared how groups performed over a series of creative tasks in which the time period increased, decreased, or stayed the same. The most creative groups were ones in which time pressure *increased* over trials. For these reasons, I routinely put a clock in the room when I work with teams. Whenever I'm conducting a brainstorming session, I always put the group on a clear, but tight, time schedule.

Now, Double It!

Ambassador Winston Lord worked for Henry Kissinger for several years as a staff aide. On several occasions, after Lord wrote a speech for Kissinger, Kissinger would tell Lord, "this is not good enough." Lord would then go back, dig deeper, and write a much better speech. On one occasion, Kissinger rejected eight of his drafts, until Lord reached a point at which he told Kissinger, "Henry, I've beaten my brains out—this is the ninth draft. I know it's the best I can do: I can't possibly improve one more word." Kissinger then replied, "In that case, now I'll read it." The point of this story is that Lord had failed to realize his potential until Kissinger rejected his attempts and sent him repeatedly back to the drawing board.

I often challenge my students and clients by first asking them to do a simple ten-minute brainstorming task. We count how many ideas they generated and score the uniqueness of their ideas. They are often quite content with their performance. Then I annoy them by asking them to double their performance in the next ten minutes. It is rather daunting task to ask for a 100 percent increase in productivity in ten minutes. I give them a few minutes or so to conspire how they can accomplish this task. What is interesting is the immediate and powerful changes teams make in their group structure. They often employ brainwriting in addition to brainstorming; they throw practicality and usefulness aside, and even set benchmarking standards for themselves (one idea every five seconds, etc.). They also *look* different. They lean in more to the group, they smile, there are bursts of laughter, and the energy level is much higher.

In my research, I have found that 93 percent of groups are able to increase their per-person productivity in the ten-minute challenge. Even more impressive, the average productivity increase is 57 percent! Just imagine what a 57 percent increase would mean in your team's productivity. What's clear to me is that *much of the time people are not nearly working to their full potential.* This is the difference between *optimizing* and *satisficing.* Herbert Simon introduced the concept of satisficing in his Nobel-Prize winning research when he observed that many people take short-cuts, meaning they do just enough to make a reasonable decision and stay out of trouble. Simon contrasted satisficing—doing just enough to get by and meet minimum goals and standards—with optimizing, which is to fully attain one's potential and use all available information and resources. When our performance is OK or satisfactory, we get comfortable. Too comfortable. A key part of creative collaboration is tapping into your creative potential and optimizing the creative ideation process. Your creative potential is much higher than you think it is. I have typically found that most people work at less than 50 percent of their actual potential.

Speedstorming

Speedstorming is a method of brainstorming not unlike speed dating. In speedstorming, groups of pairs work together for three to five minutes brainstorming. Then, like speed dating, when the allotted time is up, one person moves to the left and a new group is formed and the process starts all over again. Speedstorming combines an explicit purpose, strict time limits, and one-on-one encounters to create a dynamic setting where ideas can be explored across people from different disciplines and potential collaborators can be quickly evaluated. A direct comparison of speedstorming and brainstorming indicates that ideas from speedstorming are more technically specialized and participants are more certain in their assessment of the collaboration potential of others.

What about groups that do not have a specified time limit? When people are asked, "How do you know when to stop brainstorming?" they often look at you curiously and simply say, "When the time is up" or "When it's over." Actually, these responses are incorrect. Neither satisfaction nor enjoyment predicts how long people work. Rather, the answer is determined by the size of the group. As a general rule, persistence on a task increases as the size of the group increases. In one investigation, groups of varying sizes were given a creative task without a stop rule. The bigger the group, the longer they worked. Specifically, a comparison of individuals, dyads (two-person groups), four-person groups, and six-person groups revealed that persistence increased as the group grew larger. Thus, larger groups were about as productive as individuals and small teams, but they took longer to produce the same amount of ideas!

Flex Some Muscle

When we move our body in a way that is bringing something to us or close to us—flexing muscles, such as a bicep curl—we activate the approach centers of the brain, which are conducive to creativity. Conversely, when we push something away from us—via extending movements—we activate the avoidance centers of the brain, which are not conducive to creativity. Using insights from brain activation research, Ronald Friedman and Jens Förster had people either flex or extend their arm muscles. The flexors were more likely to reach creative insights via contextual set-breaking (i.e., thinking outside the box), restructuring (conceiving new ideas by recombining old), and expanded mental search (envisioning more categories), whereas the extenders did not. Note: they also found that if the order of the day calls for analytical reasoning (such as solving equations that have correct answers), then it is better to stretch and extend the muscles!

The reason has to do with how we think about our goals. If we are focusing on goal *promotion* and moving toward a desired state, we are more likely to be in an exploratory, risk-taking mind-set. Conversely, if we are thinking about how to avoid an undesirable or disappointing outcome, we are in a *prevention* mode. A promotion focus leads to greater creative problem solving than does a prevention focus. It is worth noting that a person in a prevention-focused state might have similar levels of creativity as in a promotion-focused state, but *only if* he or she has unfulfilled goals.

How can you induce a promotion focus in you and your team? It may be easier than you think. One method is to simply focus on the prospect of positive outcomes (e.g., winning an award, gaining recognition). In other words, a promotion focus can be temporarily induced by merely thinking about a desirable goal. For example, the team might be encouraged to think about the best possible outcome they could achieve. Alternatively, a promotion focus can also be temporarily induced through a flexing motion, such as described by the bicep study above.

Sometimes, people become excessively preoccupied with situations they want to avoid. As noted, such a prevention focus is not conducive to creativity. If you sense that yourself or others are in a preventative mind-set (obsessing about avoiding negative outcomes, such as losing a client, etc.), quickly try to focus on realistic promotion goals. When you take the time to change your cognitive focus, this causes perceptible differences in brain activation. Indeed, people who focus on the prospect of positive outcomes have greater right hemispheric activation and diminished left hemispheric activation. The right hemisphere is responsible for creative, holistic thinking, whereas the left hemisphere is engaged for analytical, rational thinking. Think of it this way: if you are attempting to generate new ideas for a product or service then the right hemisphere is needed; however, if you are attempting to solve a math or logic problem, then the left hemisphere needs to be activated.

The Road Not Taken

One type of thinking that people often engage in is *counterfactual thinking*, or thinking about what might have been had one taken a different course of action. For example, people might think about what their life might have been like if they had completed college, or taken that low-paying, but challenging job. Counterfactual thinking, as you might imagine, impairs the generation of novel ideas. However, it may have benefits for other types of noncreative problems. Thinking about what might have been prompts people to think about relations between a set of stimuli. The key here is to see connections between ideas that don't appear obvious on the surface. For this reason, thinking about what might have been improves performance on analytic tasks involving logical relationships.

Might there be a way to boost creativity even when people think about the road not taken? There is! And it involves thinking about additive, rather than subtractive counterfactuals. One way of reversing the negative effects of counterfactual thinking on creativity is to use an *additive* counterfactual in which people think of new antecedent elements to reconstruct reality. On a practical level, suppose that for example, instead of just thinking about how life might have been different if she had graduated from college, that person might be induced to think about how seeking private tutoring sessions might have allowed her to focus more on her college coursework and eventually graduate. Conversely, *subtractive* counterfactuals involve removing antecedent conditions (e.g., the person might think about how graduation prospects might have improved had she not had to work at a part-time job). Additive counterfactual mind-sets enhance performance on creative tasks but subtractive counterfactuals do not.

These results again point to the central takeway for the leader of the collaborative team: *know your goal*. Creativity is quite a different goal than analytical problem solving. We've seen in this last section that if a group is working on a complex, analytical task involving logic and rationality, counterfactual thinking is an ideal warm-up. Conversely, if a team is working on a true brainstorming task, then counterfactual thinking is not ideal.

Organizational Support for Creativity

Up to this point, I have introduced several cognitive and behavioral techniques that can significantly improve the performance of creative teams. However, it is important to note that one of the most significant predictors of team creativity is whether that team has the support of the larger organization. And the data are clear: employees who receive support for creativity from both work (supervisors and coworkers) and nonwork (family and friends) are more creative. Indeed, when team managers and team members' perceptions of organizational support are high and in agreement, team performance improves. Conversely, when team managers and team members disagree, negative affect increases and team performance suffers. The most negative effects occur when managers perceive that the team has more support than the team believes it does. Samples of senior executives identified four key norms associated with group innovation: support for risk-taking, tolerance of mistakes, teamwork, and speed of action.

There are at least three types of relevant organizational support: support from one's own work group, support from one's own supervisor, and support from the larger organization. Of all of these, it is work-group support and supervisor support that are the most instrumental in increasing creativity.

✦ Chapter Capstone

I've introduced several ideas for enhancing creativity in your next team meeting. Most of these ideas do not require significant amounts of money, but they do require you to take a risk. There is a decent chance that one or more of your colleagues will laugh at your suggestion, make fun of it, or perhaps worse, try to kill it. This is where you need to stick to your plan and make sure that you don't let the forces of inertia take over. One of my favorite lines to say is, "Look, I am committed to the success of our group. I am thrilled with how we work together, but I'm not sure we are tapping into our full potential. I want to try out some process ideas today that may sound silly, but they do have a basis in fact. Let's consider today the first of several experiments. And, if anyone wants to try something new next week, I'm all for it."

CHAPTER 8

Your Action Plan for Instigating a Creative Conspiracy

During a break in one class, one of my executive students, Mike, approached me and confided that when he was a sixteen-year-old high school student, he was diagnosed with Asperger's syndrome. His high school counselor considered this to be a fait accompli that would effectively preclude Mike from having successful relationships, and encouraged him to pursue zoology and stay away from business courses or anything that involved people skills. Needless to say, Mike was extremely upset. He decided to not follow his counselor's advice. Instead, he reappraised the bad news as a challenge and enrolled in courses on communication and nonverbal behavior, and hired a coach who taught him how to mirror body posture, maintain proper eye contact, and understand how to read between the lines in conversations. Mike is taking communication and emotional intelligence classes to this day. When he spoke to me, he was part of the senior leadership team in his company. Mike made a decision to share his diagnosis with his team. He explained to the team what he was doing to compensate for his "shortcoming" and how they could best give him feedback.

Mike had every excuse to fail at leading his team. He could have easily accepted his circumstances and put aside all aspirations of leading a creative team. But, he didn't. Mike turned the bad news into a mission.

Many of the clients who we work with will shake their heads when my colleagues and I introduce our techniques for creative collaboration and wistfully remark, "Boy I wish you had talked to me three years ago before I launched my team . . . This would have helped, but now, we are already in place." Or even worse, "I wish my boss would listen to you since he (or she) is in charge of the team, I can't do anything, especially since we have already formed . . . " It is never too late to reprocess a team—and you don't have to be the boss in order to do so! *Reprocessing* means thinking differently and strategically about anything that involves the team—meetings, communication, goals, and so on.

In this chapter, I ask you to put aside all excuses, and instead, roll up your sleeves and start instigating—just as Mike did. This chapter takes all the best practices and scientific data covered in this book and makes them work for you. We've covered a lot of detail and now the time is ripe for hatching your action plan. Below you'll find lots of concise and actionable advice. But this is the most important: *you are in the best position to be the champion of your plan.*

To have the greatest shot at success, you need to envision the plan, commit to the plan, identify those not on board, collect evidence, leverage your experience, and stop being a perfectionist!

Envision Your Plan

We have covered a lot of ground in this book. I'm not asking for you to come up with the equivalent of a Gantt chart. Nor is it necessary for you to construct a top-to-bottom plan. In fact, all you need is one thing. In my executive education courses and consulting, all I ask is that my clients and students simply pick one thing to work on each month. Not ten, not seven, and not even three. Just *one*. It does not even have to be the most important one. Give it a name so it becomes an entity. Then pull out your calendar or planner and pick out the occasions or situations in which you want to make your intention a reality. That, quite simply, is the first step.

This book will be useful for you *if you do just one thing differently next week*. So, commit to making one simple change in your behavior next week. For example, "Hey Joe, I know we are having a brainstorming meeting next week. I've read some on the subject, and I'm wondering if I could have twenty minutes during the meeting to try an experiment in creativity?" Tell your team what your vision or goal is, how you want to modify yourself to fully commit to that goal, and how they can best help to make it successful. By doing this, you unconsciously empower your team to do the same thing.

Commit to Your Plan

When I work with executives in off-site retreats, they are excited about doing things differently. However, it is not enough to simply be excited. They need to write down their plan, and then tell two people about it. They need to specify a timeline. They need to commit. I call it *creating your own virus*. You need to make your plan go viral. It starts with you and then spreads to your network.

It takes approximately ten to fourteen days for a new behavior to become a habit. This goes for everything: stopping nail-biting, starting to floss, exercising, saying "yes" instead of "yeah," etc. This means that for ten to fourteen days, you are going to have to consciously think about what you are doing. This takes energy and involves self-reflection. Most of us prefer to operate on automatic pilot and not think about our every action. To change a behavior, you need to observe yourself.

Part of committing to your plan involves identifying your co-conspirators: accomplices are absolutely critical for launching a creative conspiracy. The success of your creative conspiracy hinges on your collaborators. Who are these people? Have you briefed them on the mission?

Identify Those Not on Board

For each person on your team, indicate how they could sabotage your plan. What would they do? What would they say? People are more likely to work against you when:

- They are not informed: So inform them. Be transparent. Tell them your ultimate goals.

- They are fearful: Whatever benefits and perks they are enjoying currently may disappear. Or they might not. Be explicit about how the plan is going to personally benefit the individuals involved.

- They see losses: So focus on the gains. Focus on the half-full glass. Point to the higher-order goal.

Collect Data

Once you've determined the goal and announced it, you need to start collecting data on your change effort. Bottom line: the only way to really improve is to collect data. By this, I mean asking for feedback, measuring things, and being rigorous and unbiased. Unfortunately, most people are seriously feedback-deprived. Other people are reluctant to offer us negative feedback and so they use watered-down language because they are afraid to speak the truth. To make matters worse, we not only don't seek feedback, we actively avoid it. Seeking feedback in our organizations is like stepping on a bathroom scale. It often delivers unpleasant news and worst of all, it does not lie.

Unfortunately, dieting is easier than starting a creative conspiracy. The would-be dieter may avoid the bathroom scale, but there are other undeniable indicators that still offer feedback: the pants that don't fit, the mirror, and the way that leftover cake disappeared in one sitting. However, unaware leaders in organizations can often go for years without getting real feedback. Whether we realize it or not, we unconsciously signal to others whether we are open to feedback or conversely, that we don't want to hear anything negative. Feedback does not come to us; we need to invite it, and this means we need to signal we are working on improving our behavior. So, take notes, record dates, monitor progress. You are a role model for your team! A field study of feedback-seeking behavior of 387 managers as observed by their superiors, subordinates, and peers revealed that managers who sought negative feedback increased their accuracy of how people evaluated their work, and most important, received better evaluations of their overall performance by their managers. Conversely, those who sought positive feedback decreased their constituents' opinions of their managerial effectiveness.

Feedback is essential for the continuous improvement of any system. Unfortunately, meaningful feedback is not easy to come by, because organizations often measure the wrong things— or they don't measure anything at all. And people often distort information. In fact, studies of the ability of leaders and managers to make wise decisions have yielded relatively depressing results. The ability of decision makers to improve their judgments over time (even when they are deeply flawed) is remarkably difficult to do. People are often unwilling to look at relevant data and instead, prefer to seek data that simply confirms a rather flattering view of themselves.

So, decide in advance what behaviors and outputs you want to change and modify. Then, make sure to keep a log or journal and write down what you did, when you did it, and what the result was. Be clear and make it as scientific as possible. For example, suppose you are concerned that you are monopolizing meetings too much, cutting off others, and discouraging them from contributing. You might keep track of how often and how long you talk in meetings. Compare that to an ideal.

With regard to collecting data, keep in mind the BAT principle:

- Benchmarks: Ask for best-in-class examples. Who's really a shining example of a certain behavior? Is there a team in the organization that sets the standard for others?

- Actionable: Focus on what you can change, not what you can't change.

- Timing: Don't wait a month or even a week for feedback; get it the same day or the same hour.

The most important data will come from the "enemy"— the people who are opposed to your plan. So, the creative conspirator must collect evidence from the critics. I used to have a professor who would admonish, "Your enemy is your best friend." What Professor Tom Cook of Northwestern University was saying to us is that the people who are the most critical of your work are the people who can ultimately help you the most. I later came to realize that it is a gift when people take their time to criticize you and a curse when nobody bothers to read your work or comment on your performance. Professor Cook helped us all realize that being criticized at least means your ideas are important enough to be under discussion, rather than simply ignored.

My own experience with learning from the critics came from my own students. I was teaching a course that included an experimental new assignment, which I was quite confident would captivate students. It didn't. As a matter of fact, they hated it and started to hate everything about the class. I suppose I should not have been surprised to see my abysmal teaching ratings! After sulking for about four days, I decided to treat my failed experiment like a failed product launch. So, I sent an e-mail to several of the most outspoken students in the class inviting them to lunch and what I described as a "focus group." During lunch, I took out a large pad of paper and asked them to provide feedback on everything that should be changed about the assignment and the class. I listened and took notes. They came up with fantastic ideas, and the session was a success in brainstorming. I implemented those changes in the next term and received a completely different reaction from the students!

Your 10,000 Hours—Are You Using Them?

In 1993, psychologists Anders Ericsson, Ralf Krampe, and Clemens Tesch-Romer published research indicating that no one becomes an expert until they have studied and practiced about ten thousand hours, or approximately ten years of concentrated study. Remarkably, that seems to be true for chess players, tennis pros, business executives, and computer programmers. This looks daunting, right? However, anyone who has worked in the business world for at least five years (assuming a forty-hour workweek) has potentially accumulated enough hours to be an expert! If you consider a forty-year-old businessperson who took his first job at, say, age twenty-five and has worked eight-hour days for fifteen years, the time adds up to well over ten thousand hours. The question is: are you using the ten thousand hours of experience you have gained on the job to learn? The challenge is to start making expert sense of your business experience!

As strange as it sounds, it's very hard for us to learn from our own experience. When you are an expert in your own domain, it is sometimes hard to see a forest when each tree is absorbing your attention. Biochemistry scientists are no exception. For years, solving protein structures remained one of the most challenging problems in science. Proteins take shape from a strand of building blocks, in the form of amino acids. Genes inform the cell's protein-making machinery—the order for assembling the building blocks in a long, organized strand. When a complex protein, such as an HIV protease, comes off the assembly line, it coils and folds to form an intricate molecular machine. Unfortunately, even the most advanced computers can't predict the structure of such large proteins, because there are simply too many possible horizons. It is a bit like figuring out all possible outcomes of a chess game. So, the researchers at University of Washington did the unthinkable. They developed an online game called Foldit that embodied the protein problem and invited nonscientist gamers to play it. Within three weeks, the gamers came up with an accurate model of the protease molecule. The biochemists had been trying to create a model for more than a decade!

This example reveals that sometimes stepping outside of our domain and looking at a problem from a totally different vantage point can bring insights. We use analogical reasoning any time we use an idea from one domain to help us understand a problem in a different domain. For example, the gamers used knowledge from their own domain (gaming) to help solve a problem in a different domain (biochemistry). Unfortunately, for most of us, it is not only challenging to think outside of our own domain, it is downright inconvenient. For this reason, I applaud the biochemists for going outside their domain to get insights about their problem.

Combating the Inert Knowledge Problem

Many people have a hard time looking at their problems from a different vantage point. I'm in the business of education and I've observed that most people take learning for granted, meaning that they assume that whatever knowledge or ideas that they come into contact with in a class or on the job will be seamlessly transported to their own work situations. In short, they assume knowledge is portable. However, my research suggests that translating knowledge to the workplace may be much harder than we think. Whenever we have the knowledge to solve a problem, but fail to use it because we did not access it—or *retrieve* it—or think about it at the right time, this is a case of failed knowledge transfer. This is known as the *inert knowledge problem*—we know a lot of stuff, but we cannot access it, call it to mind, and integrate it at the right time.

This happens to people daily. For example, many students have had the unsettling feeling of failing to retrieve something that they knew while taking a test. The minute they walk out the door, the answer comes to them. Unfortunately, the answer did not come to them at the right time! Much of the knowledge we have remains frustratingly dormant or inert because we don't call it to mind at the time we need it.

It is a rather depressing fact that, left to our own devices, we can't easily transfer our knowledge. This is because our knowledge is very context-bound. Consider for example, the story of the general and the fortress. In this enigma, an evil king is holding a fortress hostage. The "good" army must invade and capture the evil king. The problem is that if enough troops are sent to capture the king, they will trip the land mines planted on the road. If fewer troops are sent, the land mines won't be tripped, but there won't be sufficient manpower to capture the king. The elegant solution is to send small numbers of troops down different roads and converge on the fortress at the same time. (By the way, very few people propose the elegant solution!)

A quite different problem is the *tumor problem*. A patient has a cancerous tumor. A high-intensity ray will kill the tumor but also destroy the surrounding healthy tissue. A low-intensity ray will protect the surrounding healthy tissue, but not kill the tumor. Very few people (10 percent) are able to successfully solve the tumor problem, which is to administer a series of low-dosage rays from different angles such that they converge on the cancerous tumor at the same time. Even when the tumor problem is preceded by the fortress problem, people have a hard timing seeing the connection (the success rates go up to 30 percent). The inability to see the *deep* connection between the two problems is another example of the *inert knowledge problem*. Indeed, once people are told the elegant solution to the tumor problem, most people regret that they did not see the parallel between the two problems.

My colleagues Dedre Gentner and Jeffrey Loewenstein and I did a decade-long investigation of the inert knowledge problem in managers. In our research, we gave managers realistic and rich business cases depicting very specific collaboration challenges and strategies. The cases contained potential for highly creative, win-win business solutions—but the solutions were in no way obvious. They required creative collaboration. For example, in one of these business scenarios, two managers are in a bitter conflict on how to divide desirable scarce resources. The antagonists considered several alternative solutions, but unfortunately none of them were mutually satisfying. Finally, a solution was concocted that involved leveraging their marked differences of opinion. One manager wanted to sell some property that was jointly owned because he feared that real estate prices were falling. The other partner did not want to sell the property because she was much more optimistic about real estate value. We then presented a creative, "elegant" solution to the problem in which the parties settled on a contingent contract that was based on future real estate prices.

A week later, we challenged the managers (who had read these business cases and solutions) with a negotiation case in a very different industry in which the parties had different views of the future. This would have been the perfect opportunity to apply what they had learned a week ago, right? Wrong! The majority of managers did not recall the business case they had read a week earlier and instead settled for a suboptimal solution. In short, they satisficed! This is a perfect example of the inert knowledge problem—the managers had solutions but didn't use them! What's more, when we reminded them about the previous week's cases, they were upset that they had not used what they had learned!

Positive Transfer

Ideally, managers need to engage in *positive transfer*, which is to call to mind knowledge that is ideally suited to the problem at hand. In positive transfer, the superficial detail is often unrelated, but the deep concepts are related. To return to our example of the tumor problem, if the student had recalled the fortress problem, this would be an example of positive transfer. At a superficial level, there is no apparent relationship between a king holding a fortress hostage and a cancer growing inside a patient. But at a deep level, attacking the king by traveling on different roads that converge on the fortress at the same time is deeply analogous to attacking a cancerous tumor via radiation that emanates from different angles that converge on the tumor at the same time.

Another example of positive transfer occurs in the movie *A Beautiful Mind*. Nobel Prize–winning mathematician John Nash, played by Russell Crowe, has a fascinating moment of positive transfer when he sees a deep parallel to the problem of how to pick up women in a bar and how to negotiate with multiple people so that all interests can be met! Nash argues that if all of his friends "go for the blonde," they will in effect block one another's efforts, and in the end, none of them will succeed; furthermore, the other women will reject them as well because they have been insulted. So Nash proposes that they can achieve their ultimate goal of securing a date if they each approach a different woman—and all stay away from the attractive blonde. And in the case of the tumor and fortress examples, the student who successfully solves the fortress problem will be reminded of her solution when she is confronted with the tumor problem.

False Transfer

One implication of the inert knowledge problem is that sometimes we call the wrong knowledge to mind. This is what is known as *false transfer*. I had a student who was (wrongly) reminded of a given company case example that was superficially similar to the topic we were discussing. The key focus of our discussion was win-win negotiations. I planned to challenge the students with a very complex international business case loosely based on the Euro Disney negotiations. I was distributing the case when one student raised his hand and glibly commented that the entire class had already done the case. I immediately panicked. What do I do for the next three hours, I wondered? My pulse raced and my breathing became choppy. My worst nightmare had come true—the students had already done the case! Now what? I collected myself and asked the student to describe the case. The student began describing a marketing case that happened to involve Euro Disney but in fact had no relevance to win-win collaborative negotiation. It was a case that was fundamentally different at its core, but on the surface appeared similar. In short, the student had mentally "filed" the marketing case under "Disney" rather than "marketing segmentation"—an example of negative transfer. False transfer often happens when people store knowledge in a superficial fashion. In this case, the student had not remembered the marketing principles inherent in the case, but had remembered the superficial information. In my own classes on leadership, negotiation, creativity, teams, and decision making, I am careful to provide at least two to three examples that illustrate the key point. This is because a single case will create an unhelpful context dependence.

The question is: how to make the knowledge and insights we possess more readily available when we need them? How can we make the fundamental principle, takeaway, or learning point the central focus of our long-term memory rather than superficial—and largely irrelevant information? And, what can you do to increase your ability to engage in optimal learning and positive transfer?

Learn Actively, Not Passively

I tell my clients to read their favorite books and magazines with a specific purpose in mind; similarly, I tell my doctoral students to read journal articles with the goal of thinking about how the theory and findings influence their research. I also tell my PhD students that everything they write should be done with the goal of getting published. Another way of learning actively is to say it, communicate it, explain it, and use it. In other words, when you read an interesting book or hear of a good idea, put it into your own words and tell somebody about it. Learn to answer that person's questions. This creates a learning orientation. Giles Hirst and his colleagues studied twenty-five R&D teams in a pharmaceutical company and measured their learning orientation and their creativity. On average, employees had worked for the company for three years and were responsible for developing new and creative therapeutic treatments and technology initiatives. The individual employees completed a survey regarding their work in detail, and each employee's direct supervisor was asked to complete a different survey that rated each R&D team's creativity based on the tasks the employees were hired to do. Hirst found that teams with a strong learning orientation were more creative.

Tell Stories

It is a scientific fact that people remember narrative more than facts. We grow up hearing stories, remembering stories, and enjoying stories, but most of us are lousy at telling our own stories. We need to work on that. People remember stories much longer than they remember information delivered in a boring, factual way. For example, entrepreneurs construct meaning during the early stages of a new venture by using analogical and metaphorical reasoning. So, when learning a new idea or concept, think of at least two examples or stories that illustrate the idea. Then compare them and derive the core idea. In one of my studies, my colleagues and I experimented with giving people one versus two stories to illustrate a point, and the effects were dramatic. Namely, people who had read two stories were able to derive a key theme or idea. Their learning trace—their own mental takeaway from reading the stories—was deeper and contained the critical core of the idea. In contrast, those who had only read one story had a weaker learning trace that contained a lot of irrelevant facts. We also examined whether just giving students the essence of a story—i.e., the takeaway point—would be effective in increasing knowledge transfer. It wasn't. Rather, we found that the key to long-term knowledge transfer is to have the student, manager, team member—the learner—do the mental work of deriving the core principle. For this reason, I ask my students to recall the best lecture they ever attended—in college, grad school, company training session, and so on. Then I ask them what they remember that made it so great. Inevitably, it was a story told by the speaker that illustrated a point that profoundly connected with the life of that student.

Dig Through Your Own Database

Your meeting today with the new chairperson reminded you of what? Your brainstorming session today was similar to what? Use multiple examples to make sense of everything you learn. Don't file away facts by remembering one situation, think of two (or more) and then pull out the common denominator. This leads to deep learning as opposed to superficial learning.

Stop Being a Perfectionist

Each one of us is a work in progress, and we will never arrive at a final point of completion. In short, you will never be perfect. Neither will I. But we will have tried, and, in trying, we will have been part of the largest conspiracy in our lives: the conspiracy of how to improve ourselves. We all need to work on how to improve ourselves every day. Having a goal of self-improvement gives each day a purpose. Each one of us needs to be working on how to improve ourselves; we cannot stay in place while our team improves.

How You Can Sabotage Your Own Plan

You are in a unique position to either be the greatest champion for your plan or its biggest saboteur. As a start, think about a recent team experience in which you tried to do something you thought would help the team, but—alas—it backfired, failed, or simply did not catch on. If you have to pinpoint one reason why your change effort was not successful, what would you say? Be specific. If you are like most people, you said something like, "The personalities on my team are dysfunctional" or "Certain team members never want to listen to me" or "I ran out of time" or "I did not have a sufficient budget" or "The client was difficult to work with." There is a common thread among these explanations that can be simply summed up in the sentence, "It is not my fault that I did not succeed." All of these explanations are what psychologists label *external attributions*, precisely because we are blaming something or somebody other than ourselves. When we externalize, we essentially give up. When we give up on our team, we give up on ourselves. The depressing reality is that 95 percent of managers make external attributions when they attempt to determine the cause of poor team performance.

Interestingly, when we flip the question and ask managers to think of a team experience that was highly successful, 95 percent of these same people cite internal factors—"I'm a great leader" they often say, or "My instincts are very good" or "I have good people skills." Blaming away failures and taking credit for success is a highly self-congratulatory pattern. Psychologists call it an *egocentric* pattern.

Let's look more carefully at these patterns. Not surprisingly, they impact mood and well-being: depressed people are less likely to externalize. So, there is some psychological benefit to blaming others, but it comes at a potentially serious cost—namely, the big problem is that our ability to learn and adapt is severely curtailed when we externalize our shortcomings.

Create a Self-Fulfilling Prophecy

In one famous experiment, teachers were told that certain children in their class would blossom intellectually over the academic year, whereas certain other children would show a normal developmental pattern in the classroom. During the course of the year, the children who were expected to bloom in fact did! Their test scores and performance were markedly higher than the others. Not surprising, right? Well, not unless it was completely random which children were described as bloomers. In fact, there were no discernible differences among the children at the beginning of the year, but the teachers were led to believe that certain children would bloom. This led to a self-fulfilling chain of events, which ultimately led to a random group of children truly improving—all because of a belief on the part of the teacher.

Let's go back to our example of the failed team intervention. Suppose the leader decides that it is the dysfunctional personalities of two team members that have caused the team to fail. To be specific, the leader regards these people as ego-driven, controlling, and opposed to change. Further, our leader has suspected this for quite some time—years, in fact—and has been casually collecting data on these team members' deplorable behavior. The conclusion? The leader had developed a personal theory that conveniently explained the team's failure and was not open to testing the accuracy of that theory. In fact, even when presented with evidence that his explanation for the problem team members was most likely in error, the leader turned a blind eye.

One study illustrates how powerful our perceptions are in changing reality. In this investigation, men were instructed to have phone conversations with women. The theory being tested was the self-fulfilling prophecy—if men believed they were talking to a gorgeous woman, the two would hit it off, so to speak, and would be likely to go on a date. Men were given photos of the women they were allegedly speaking with. Some photos were of "attractive" women; some "plain"—based on ratings made beforehand by a separate sample of people. (Of course, the photos men were given were not actually the person with whom they were talking to on the phone.) The conversations engaged in by men who thought they were speaking with a particularly attractive woman were fundamentally different from those of men who thought they were speaking with a plain woman. Even more surprisingly, the women began to act in fundamentally different ways as a function of how they were being conversed with—despite the fact that they all were judged by outsiders to be equally attractive! Women who spoke to men who believed they were beautiful began to converse more fluently, laugh more, and in general exhibit better social skills. This study and countless others reveal how we can create our own reality by unconsciously treating others as we expect them to behave. Perhaps it is for this reason that creative people are more open to the possibility that people can change, and they often describe the behavior of others as not due so much to dysfunctional personality traits, but rather, situational pressures. Creative people are not universalists—rather, they are situationists. This is hugely important because you can't change someone's personality, but you can change the situation.

Incidentally, the same goes when we are attempting to explain the causes of our own behavior. The data are in: people who feel that they are able to improve potential failure are more creative than people who don't think they can improve.

Making Anxiety Work for You

If you put a dog in a green room and give it electric shocks, the dog quickly learns to avoid that room. But what if the green room is your action plan for creative collaboration and people are so afraid of past experiences that they won't try anything new? Worse yet, what if *you* are the dog in the green room?

We all know that dogs are smart, or at least adaptive. Once they are shocked (punished) for doing something new, they will continue to avoid new behaviors, even when the shock is totally removed. So, if you've been punished in the past for trying something new, then how do you get past those negative experiences and commit yourself to change? According to management scientist guru Edgar Schein, for change to happen, your *type 2 anxiety* needs to be greater than your *type 1 anxiety*. Think of type 1 anxiety as the anxiety you feel when you are asked to learn something new or try something different. For example, remember that vacation when someone asked you to try paragliding, and you were intrigued, but also anxious? Type 1 anxiety is the feeling associated with an inability or unwillingness to learn something new because it appears too difficult, disruptive, or risky. It is what leads people to fear change.

Type 2 anxiety is different. Think of it as the haunting feeling that whatever you are doing now is just not good enough or won't work in the long term. Type 2 anxiety is the feeling that your current way of doing things is not enough, no longer working, or just not satisfying. The opposite of type 2 anxiety is complacency. Actually, I hope that after reading this book, you are feeling a certain amount of anxiety—about how the current state of affairs is not quite optimal and how there are clear and concrete best practices you can introduce to improve the performance of your team. That type of restlessness—type 2 anxiety—is the ideal fuel for change.

✐ Chapter Capstone

The creative conspiracy begins with one simple idea, followed by a commitment that the next meeting with your team will be different. There is a very good chance the meeting will be more productive as a result of your intervention. It is unlikely that what you do at that meeting will negatively affect your team in the long run. If your plan does backfire, tell the team what your intention was and ask how that goal might have been better accomplished. In fact, groups that reflect on how they work, what they do wrong, and what they do right perform better than groups who don't reflect. Thus, by orchestrating such a conversation, your team is now part of the conspiracy. Ask your team if you—or, for that matter, anyone else—can have a hand in organizing the next week's meeting.

A creative conspiracy begins with one person—hopefully, you—thinking perceptively about how to ignite your team. Think of your goal as an operation—a mission—that you have been asked to do. You can't abandon the mission. But you can change how you get there.

There will be clues and signs and keys hidden in your organization that you must decode. What looks to be a lazy team member is actually a person who is dying to be put on assignment. The boring white wall in the seminar room can be temporarily transformed into a hotbed of activity via sticky notes, smelly pens, and some hoopla. The negative response you received from the governing body regarding your team's proposal can be viewed as a message to be decoded and acted on in a different, clandestine fashion. If you have just taken on your first job or first leadership role, great. And for those of us wondering what we've been doing for the last decade and how we can possibly jump into action at this point, consider the creative conspiracy your second act. You are being called to set the stage.

NOTES

The initial numbers refer to page numbers in this book and italicized phrases identify sentences with citations.

Introduction

5. *In a substantial data set:* L.J. Kornish and K.T. Ulrich, "Opportunity Spaces in Innovation: Empirical Analysis of Large Samples of Ideas," *Management Science* 57, no. 1 (2011), 107–128.

7. *Distrust can increase:* J. Mayer and T. Mussweiler, "Suspicious Spirits, Flexible Minds: When Distrust Enhances Creativity," *Journal of Personality and Social Psychology* 101, no. 6 (2011): 1262–1277.

7. *Thinking creatively leads:* F. Gino and D. Ariely, "The Dark Side of Creativity: Original Thinkers Can Be More Dishonest," *Journal of Personality and Social Psychology* 102, no. 3 (2012): 445–459.

8. *People who learn passively:* F. Gino, L. Argote, E. Miron-Spektor, and G. Todorova, "First, Get Your Feet Wet: The Effects of Learning from Direct and Indirect Experience on Team Creativity," *Organizational Behavior and Human Decision Processes* 111, no. 2 (2010): 102–115.

Chapter 1

12. *To summarize succinctly:* S. Cain, "The Rise of the New Groupthink," *New York Times*, January 13, 2012.

14. *Nominal groups outperformed real groups:* Quality was measured as the "percentage of good ideas" as judged by independent experts who did not know whose ideas they were evaluating; see M. Diehl and W. Stroebe, "Productivity Loss in Brainstorming Groups: Toward a Solution of a Riddle," *Journal of Personality and Social Psychology* 53 (1987): 497–509.

14. *For example, teams that build:* K. Girotra, C. Terwiesch, and K.T. Ulrich, "Idea Generation and the Quality of the Best Idea," *Management Science* 56, no. 4 (2010): 591–605.

15. *Paul Paulus and his team:* P. Paulus, T. Nakui, V.L. Putman, and V.R. Brown, "Effects of Task Instructions and Brief Breaks on Brainstorming," *Group Dynamics* 10, no. 3 (2006): 206–219; V.L. Putman and P.B. Paulus, "Brainstorming, Brainstorming Rules, and Decision Making," *Journal of Creative Behavior* 43, no. 1 (2009): 23–39.

15. *For example, in one provocative field investigation:* J.R. Barker, "Tightening the Iron Cage: Concertive Control in Self-Managing Teams," *Administrative Science Quarterly* 38 (1993): 408–437.

16. *Lilach Sagiv and colleagues compared:* L. Sagiv, S. Arieli, J. Goldenberg, and A. Goldschmidt, "Structure and Freedom in Creativity: The Interplay Between Externally Imposed Structure and Personal Cognitive Style," *Journal of Organizational Behavior* 31, no. 8 (2010): 1086–1110.

16. *To test this assumption:* P.B. Paulus, N.W. Kohn, and L.E. Arditti, "Effects of Quantity and Quality Instructions on Brainstorming," *Journal of Creative Behavior* 4, no. 1 (2011): 38–46.

17. *According to Catmull:* E. Catmull, "How Pixar Fosters Collective Creativity," *Harvard Business Review*, September 2008, 64–73.

18. *However, taking a break:* N.W. Kohn and S.M. Smith, "Collaborative Fixation: Effects of Others' Ideas on Brainstorming," *Journal of Applied Cognitive Psychology* 35, no. 3 (in press): 359–371.

18. *One night, he dreamed:* D. Barrett, "Answers in Your Dreams," *Scientific American Mind*, May 2011, 27–33.

18. *Steven Smith and Steven Blankenship:* S.M. Smith and S.E. Blankenship, "Incubation and the Persistence of Fixation in Problem Solving," *American Journal of Psychology* 104 no. (1991): 61–87.

19. *Furthermore, in recent decades:* S. Cain, "The Rise of the New Groupthink," *New York Times*, January 15, 2012.

19. *And 76 percent of the worst programmers:* T. DeMarco and T. Lister, *Programmers Performance and the Effects of the Workplace* (Los Alamitos, CA: IEEE Computer Society Press, 1985).

20. *She found that hybrid structures:* K. Girotra, C. Terwiesch, and K.T. Ulrich, "Idea Generation and the Quality of the Best Idea," *Management Science* 56, no. 4 (2010): 591–605.

20. *Paul Paulus and his research team:* J. Baruah and P.B. Paulus, "Effects of Training on Idea Generation in Groups," *Small Group Research* 39, no. 5 (2008): 523–541.

21. *People who are pro-self:* B. Beersma and C.K.W. DeDreu, "Conflict's Consequences: Effects of Social Motives on Post-Negotiation Creative and Convergent Group Functioning and Performance," *Journal of Personality and Social Psychology* 89, no. 3 (2005): 358–374; J.A. Goncalo and B.M. Staw, "Individualism-Collectivism and Group Creativity," *Organizational Behavior and Human Decision Processes* 100, no. 1 (2006): 96–109.

22. *In fact, it is better to be aroused:* C.K.W. DeDreu, M. Baas, and B.A. Nijstad, "Hedonic Tone and Activation Level in the Mood-Creativity

Link: Toward a Dual Pathway to Creativity Model," *Journal of Personality and Social Psychology* 94, no. 5 (2008): 739–756.

34. *As a general rule of thumb:* R. A. Hackman, *Leading Teams: Setting the Stage for Great Performance* (Boston: Harvard Business School Press, 2002).

Chapter 2

37. *Sociologist Matthew Brashears:* M. Brashears, "Small Networks and High Isolation? A Reexamination of American Discussion Networks," *Social Networks* 33, no. 4 (2011): 331–341.

38. *The frequency of virtual communication:* A. Lenhart, "Teens, Texting and Smartphones," *Pew Internet and American Life Project*, March 19, 2012, www.pewinternet.org.

38. *Even though people consider:* S. Keri, "Solitary Minds and Social Capital: Latent Inhibition, General Intellectual Functions and Social Network Size Predict Creative Achievements," *Psychology of Aesthetics, Creativity, and the Arts* (2011).

38. *E-mail and other forms:* New York Times, as reported in THE WEEK, July 20, 2012, page 36.

38. *In one study, information technology workers:* Monitor On Psychology, July–August, 2012, page 16.

38. *Many of my clients:* New York Times, as reported in THE WEEK, July 27, 2012, page 4.

40. *Psychologically, there are two major reasons:* C.A. Insko, R.H. Smith, M.D. Alicke, J. Wade, and S. Taylor, "Conformity and Group Size: The Concern with Being Right and the Concern with Being Liked," *Personality and Social Psychology Bulletin* 11, no. 1 (1985): 41–50.

40. *Psychologist Stanley Schachter:* S. Schachter, "Deviation, Rejection and Communication," *Journal of Abnormal and Social Psychology* 46 (1951): 190–207.

41. *When we mirror others:* A.D. Galinsky, G. Ku, and C.S. Wang, "Perspective-Taking and Self-Other Overlap: Fostering Social Bonds and Facilitating Social Coordination," *Group Processes Intergroup Relations* 8, no. 2 (2005): 109–124.

41. *Unfortunately, the downside:* C.E. Ashton-James and T.L. Chartrand, "Social Cues for Creativity: The Impact of Behavioral Mimicry on Convergent and Divergent Thinking," *Journal of Experimental Social Psychology* 45, no. 4 (2009): 1036–1040.

41. *In contrast, people responding:* M. Isaacs and K. Chen, "Presence/Absence of an Observer in a Word Association Test," *Journal of Personality Assessment* 55, no. 1 and 2 (1990): 41–51.

41. *The following conditions:* R.S. Feldman, *Social Psychology* (Englewood Cliffs, NJ: Prentice Hall, 1995).

42. *One study examined how conformity:* J. Goncalo and M. Duguid, "Follow the Crowd in a New Direction: When Conformity Pressure Facilitates Group Creativity (and When It Does Not)," in *Organizational Behavior and Human Decision Process* 118, no. 10 (2012).

43. *For example, they talk about:* T. Gross, "'Imagine' That: Fostering Creativity in the Workplace," *Fresh Air*, National Public Radio, March 21, 2012.

43. *Free riding is the number-one complaint:* L. Thompson, Leading High Impact Teams, executive program, Kellogg School of Management, 2012).

43. *For example, just over 1 percent:* Corporation for Public Broadcasting Annual Report, Fiscal Year 2009, www.cpb.org.

43. *As it turns out, people in groups:* W.J. Boyes, W.S. Mounts, and C. Sowell, "Restaurant Tipping: Free Riding, Social Acceptance, and Gender Differences," *Journal of Applied Psychology* 34 (2004): 2616–2628.

44. *In one study, when preschoolers:* E. Nagourney, "Behavior: More Children, Eating More Graham Crackers," *New York Times*, February 20, 2007, nytimes.com.

44. *Whether the task is shouting:* S. Karau and K. Williams, "Social Loafing: A Meta-Analytic Review and Theoretical Integration," *Journal of Personality and Social Psychology* 65, no. 4 (1993): 681–706.

46. *Instead of competition:* M.C. Roy, S. Gauvin, and M. Limayem, "Electronic Group Brainstorming: The Role of Feedback on Productivity," *Small Group Research,* 27, no. 2 (1996): 215–247.

47. *Wearing similar t-shirts:* S. Gaetner, M. Rust, G. Mottola, et al., "Reducing Intergroup Bias: Elements of Intergroup Cooperation," *Interpersonal Relations and Group Process* 76, no. 3 (1999): 388–402.

47. *When less similar linguistic terms:* L. Scissors, A. Gill, K. Geraghty, et al., "In CMC We Trust: The Role of Similarity," *Proceedings of the 27th International Conference on Human Factors in Computing Systems* (April 7, 2009): 527–536.

47. *In short, focusing on the collective identity:* M.B. Brewer and R.M. Kramer, "Choice Behavior in Social Dilemmas: Effects of Social Identity, Group Size, and Decision Framing," *Journal of Personality and Social Psychology* 50, no. 3 (1986): 543–549.

48. *This also explains:* C.C. Chen, X.P. Chen, and J.R. Meindle, "How Can Cooperation Be Fostered? The Cultural Effects of Individualism-Collectivism," *Academy of Management Review* 23, no. 2 (1998): 285–304.

48. *I use a dialogue-based peer review:* Dispute Resolution Research Center, Kellogg School of Management, http://negotiationexercises.com/Details.aspx?ItemID=101.

49. *It is worth noting:* P.J. Silvia and A.G. Phillips, "Self-Awareness, Self-Evaluation and Creativity," *Personality and Social Psychology Bulletin* 30, no. 8 (2004): 1009–1017.

52. *For example, people who have been:* P.B. Paulus, M.T. Dzindolet, G. Poletes, and M.L. Camacho, "Perception of Performance in Group Brainstorming: The Illusion of Group Productivity," *Personality and Social Psychology Bulletin* 19 (1993): 78–89; W. Stroebe, M. Diehl, and G. Abakoumkin, "The Illusion of Group Efficacy," *Personality and Social Psychology Bulletin* 18, no. 5 (1992): 643–650.

52. *However, these brainstorming groups:* B. Mullen, C. Johnson, and E. Salas, "Productivity Loss in Brainstorming Groups: A Meta-Analytic Integration," *Basic and Applied Social Psychology* 12, no. 1 (1991): 3–23.

53. *Even though binging:* R. Franke and J. Kaul, "Hawthorne Experiments: First Statistical Interpretations," *American Sociological Review* 43, no. 5 (1978): 623–643.

53. *In one nursing home:* N. Foner, *The Caregiving Dilemma: Work in an American Nursing Home* (Berkeley, CA: *University of California Press,* 1995).

54. *Moreover, people are more likely to harm:* C. Lam, G.S. Van der Vegt, F. Walter, and X. Huang, "Harming High Performers: A Social Comparison Perspective on Interpersonal Harming in Work Teams," *Journal of Applied Psychology* 96, no. 3 (2011): 588–601.

54. *Think of it this way:* J.M. Levine, "Reaction to Opinion Deviance In Small Groups," in *Psychology of Group Influence,* ed. P.B. Paulus, 2nd ed. (Hillsdale, NJ: Erlbaum, 1989), 187–231.

54. *Accordingly, low-productivity people:* J.J. Seta, "The Impact of Comparison Processes on Coactors' Task Performance," *Journal of Personality and Social Psychology* 42, no. 2 (1982): 281–291.

54. *Conversely, high-productivity people:* N. Kerr and R. McCoun, "Role Expectations in Social Dilemmas: Sex Roles and Task Motivation in Groups," *Journal of Personality and Social Psychology* 49 (1985): 1547–1556

54. *As this suggests:* P.B. Paulus and M.T. Dzindolet, "Social Influence Processes in Group Brainstorming," *Journal of Personality and Social Psychology* 64 (1993): 575–586.

54. *In sum, several investigations:* P.B. Paulus and V.R. Brown, "A Simple Dynamic Model of Social Factors in Group Brainstorming," *Small Group Research* 27, no. 1 (1996): 91–114; Paulus and Dzindolet, "Social Influence Processes in Group Brainstorming."

55. *For example, the performance of a group:* Paulus and Dzindolet, "Social Influence Processes in Group Brainstorming."

55. *For example, in one investigation, the productivity gap:* Ibid.

55. *Thus pressure from outside a group:* J.J. Seta, P.B. Paulus, and J.K. Schkade, "Effects of Group Size and Proximity Under Cooperative and Competitive Conditions," *Journal of Personality and Social Psychology* 34 (1976): 47–53; J.J. Seta, C.E. Seta, and S. Donaldson, "The Impact of Comparison Processes on Coactors' Frustration and Willingness to Expend Effort," *Personality and Social Psychology Bulletin* 17 (1991): 560–568.

55. *Thus, my best advice on how to raise:* J. Munkes and M. Diehl, "Matching or Competition? Performance Comparison Processes in an Idea Generation Task," *Group Processes and Intergroup Relations* 6, no. 3 (2003): 305–320.

56. *In a study conducted at the University of California:* G. Mark, V. Gonzalez, and J. Harris, "No Task Left Behind? Examining the Nature of Fragmented Work," working paper, (Irvine, CA: University of California), 2005.

56. *It is not surprising:* V. Brown and P.B. Paulus, "A Simple Dynamic Model of Social Factors in Group Brainstorming," *Small Group Research* 27, no. 1 (1996): 91–114.

56. *The delay between idea generation and articulation:* B.A. Nijstad, W. Stroebe, and H.F.M. Lodewijkx, "Production Blocking and Idea Generation: Does Blocking Interfere With Cognitive Processes?" *Journal of Experimental Social Psychology* 39, no. 6 (2003): 531–548.

57. *This delay interfered:* Ibid.

57. *Taking turns interferes:* B.A. Nijstad and W. Stroebe, "How the Group Affects the Mind: A Cognitive Model of Idea Generation in Groups," *Personality and Social Psychology Review* 10, no. 3 (2006): 186–213.

57. *People who are regularly bombarded:* E. Ophir, C.I. Nass, and A.D. Wagner, "Cognitive Control in Media Multitaskers," *Proceedings of the National Academy of Sciences* 106 (2009): 15583–15587.

58. *There has been a 10 percent:* "Going the distance: Online Education in the United States, 2011," The Sloan Consortium, http://sloanconsortium. org/publications/survey/going_distance_2011.

58. *By not feeling that their questions:* J. Pierce, "Shy Students Should Be Able to Tweet Their Teacher in Class, Study Finds," *Courier Mail* [Australia], January 16, 2012, couriermail.com.

59. *We call this the:* T. Menon and L. Thompson, "Don't Hate Me Because I'm Beautiful: Self-Enhancing Biases in Threat Appraisal," *Organizational Behavior and Human Decision Processes* 104, no. 1 (2007): 45–60.

60. The *fear of negative evaluation scale:* D. Watson, and R. Friend, "Measurement of Social-Evaluative Anxiety," *Journal of Consulting and Clinical Psychology* 33 (1969): 448–457.

60. *Here are a few items:* M.R. Leary, "A Brief Version of the Fear of Negative Evaluation Sale," *Personality and Social Psychology Bulletin* 9, no. 3 (1983): 371–375.

61. *An average score:* Ibid.

Chapter 3

65. *An investigation of scientific:* S. Wuchty, B. Jones, and B. Uzzi, "The Increasing Dominance of Teams in Production of Knowledge," *Science* 316 (2007): 1036–1039.

65. *Similarly, James Adams:* A. James, "Scientific Teams and Institutional Collaborations: Evidence from U.S. Universities, 1981–1999," *Research Policy* 34, no. 3 (2005): 259–285.

65. *Gerald Marschke found:* G. Marchke, *Teams in R&D: Evidence from US Investor Data*, Bonn, Germany: Institute for the Study of Labor (March 29, 2011), iza.org.

67. *Creative members enhance:* E. Miron-Spektor, M. Erez, and E. Naveh, "The Effect of Conformist and Attentive-to-Detail Members on Team Innovation: Reconciling the Innovation Paradox," *Academy of Management Journal* 54, no. 4 (2011): 740–760.

67. *In one study:* R. Mauro, A. Pierro, L. Mannetti, E.T. Higgins, and A.W. Kruglanski, "The Perfect Mix: Regulatory Complementarity and the Speed-Accuracy Balance in Group Performance," *Psychological Science* 20 (2009): 681–685.

68. *The results indicated that:* A. Miura and M. Hida, "Synergy Between Diversity and Similarity in Group-Idea Generation," *Small Group Research* 35 (2004): 540–64.

68. *One investigation compared:* P.L. McLeod, S.A. Lobel and T.H. Cox, Jr., "Ethnic Diversity and Creativity in Small Groups," *Small Group Research* 27, no. 2 (1996), 248–264.

68. *In another study, European Americans:* A.K. Leung and C. Chiu, "Multicultural Experience, Idea Receptiveness, and Creativity," *Journal of Cross-Cultural Psychology* 41, no. 5 (2010), 723–741.

68. *However, other investigations:* S.B.F. Paletz, K. Peng, M. Erez, and C. Maslach, "Ethnic Composition and Its Differential Impact on Group Processes in Diverse Teams," *Small Group Research* 35, no. 2 (2004): 128–157.

68. *Teams with greater educational specialization heterogeneity:* S.J. Shin, and J. Zhou, "When Is Educational Specialization

Heterogeneity Related to Creativity in Research and Development Teams? Transformational Leadership as a Moderator," *Journal of Applied Psychology* 92, no. 6 (2007): 1709–1721.

69. *In a landmark study of creativity:* K. Dunbar, "How Scientists Think: Online Creativity and Conceptual Change in Science," in *Creative Thought: An Investigation of Conceptual Structures and Processes*, ed. T.B. Ward, S.M. Smith, and S. Vaid (Washington, DC: American Psychological Association, 1997), 461–493.

69. *Whereas the average contributions:* J.S. Valacich, B.C. Wheeler, B.E. Mennecke, and R. Wachter, "The Effects of Numerical and Logical Group Size on Computer-Mediated Idea Generation," *Organizational Behavior and Human Decision Processes* 62, no. 3 (1995): 318–329.

69. *For example, studies of teams:* M.J. Pearsall, A.P.J. Ellis, and J.M. Evans, "Unlocking the Effects of Gender Faultlines on Team Creativity: Is Activation the Key?" *Journal of Applied Psychology* 93, no. 1 (2008): 225–234.

70. *General cognitive ability:* N.R. Kuncel, S.A. Hezlett, and D.S. Ones, "Academic Performance, Career Potential, Creativity, and Job Performance: Can One Construct Predict Them All?" *Journal of Personality and Social Psychology* 86, no. 1 (2004): 148–161; S.J. Dollinger, "'Standardized Minds' or Individuality? Admissions Tests and Creativity Revisited," *Psychology of Aesthetics, Creativity, and the Arts.*

70. *For example, in one study:* J.S. Valacich, B.C. Wheeler, B.E. Mennecke, and R. Wachter, "The Effects of Numerical and Logical Group Size on Computer-Mediated Idea Generation," *Organizational Behavior and Human Decision Processes* 62, no. 3 (1995): 318–329.

70. *In one investigation, narcissists:* J.A. Goncalo, F.J. Flynn, and S.H. Kim, "Are Two Narcissists Better Than One? The Link Between Narcissism, Perceived Creativity and Creative Performance," *Personality and Social Psychology Bulletin* 36, no. 11 (2010): 1485–1495.

70. *Narcissists are more likely:* Narcissistic personality quiz, 2012, psychcentral.com.

72. *Creative people are less likely:* P. Bierly, R.W. Kolodinsky, and B.J. Charette, "Understanding the Complex Relationship Between Creativity and Ethical Ideologies," *Journal of Business Ethics* 86, no. 1 (2009): 101–112.

72. *Teams produce more ideas:* M.N. Bechtoldt, C.K.W. DeDreu, B.A. Nijstad, and H.S. Choi, "Motivated Information Processing, Social Tuning, and Group Creativity," *Journal of Personality and Social Psychology* 99, no. 4 (2010): 622–637.

72. *The people high in epistemic motivation:* G.A. Van Kleef, C. Anastasopoulou, and B.A. Nijstad, "Can Expressions of Anger Enhance

Creativity? A Test of the Emotions as Social Information (EASI) Model," *Journal of Experimental Social Psychology* 46, no. 6 (2010): 1042–1048.

72. *People who are high in epistemic motivation:* M.M. Thompson, M.E. Naccarato, and K.E. Parker, "Assessing Cognitive Need: The Development of the Personal Need for Structure and the Personal Fear of Invalidity Scales," paper presented at the annual meeting of the Canadian Psychological Association, Halifax, Nova Scotia, 1989.

73. *The idealistic person:* D.R. Forsyth, "Judging the Morality of Business Practices: The Influence of Personal Moral Philosophies," *Journal of Business Ethics* 11, no. 5–6 (1992):, 461–470; D.R. Forsyth, J.L. Nye, and K. Kelley, "Idealism, Relativism, and the Ethic of Caring," *Journal of Psychology* 122, no. 3 (1988): 243–248.

73. *Idealists are people:* D.P. Forsyth, "A Taxonomy of Ethical Ideologies," *Journal of Personality and Social Psychology* 39, no. 1 (1980): 175–184.

73. *Paul Bierly and his colleagues:* P. Bierly, R.W. Kolodinsky, and B.J. Charette, "Understanding the Complex Relationship between Creativity and Ethical Ideologies," *Journal of Business Ethics* 86, no. 1 (2009): 101–112.

74. *The most creative achievers in middle age:* R. Helson and S. Srivastava, "Creative and Wise People: Similarities, Differences, and How They Develop," *Personality and Social Psychology Bulletin* 28, no. 10 (2002): 1430–1440.

74. *Teams composed primarily of people:* M. Baer, G.A. Oldham, G.C Jacobsen, and A.B. Hollingshead, "The Personality Composition of Teams and Creativity: The Moderating Role of Team Creative Confidence," *Journal of Creative Behavior* 4, no. 42 (2008): 255–282.

74. *Moreover, when non-anxious people:* L.M. Camacho and P.B. Paulus, "The Role of Social Anxiousness in Group Brainstorming," *Journal of Personality and Social Psychology* 68, no. 6 (1995): 1071–1080.

75. *Some of the teams were composed:* A. Chirumbolo, L. Mannetti, A. Pierro, A. Areni, and A.W. Kruglanski, "Motivated Closed-Mindedness and Creativity in Small Groups," *Small Group Research* 36, no. 1 (2005): 59–82; C.K.W. DeDreu and B.A. Nijstad, "Mental set and creative thought in social conflict: Threat rigidity versus motivated focus," *Journal of Personality and Social Psychology* 95, no. 3 (2008): 648–661.

76. *In a provocative study:* M. Baer, "The Strength of Weak Ties Perspective on Creativity: A Comprehensive Examination and Extension," *Journal of Applied Psychology* 95, no. 3 (2010): 592–601.

76. *Moreover, teams whose members have different levels:* M.C. Schilpzand, D.M. Herold, and C.E. Shalley, "Members' Openness to Experience and Teams' Creative Performance," *Small Group Research* 42, no. 1 (2011): 55–76.

76. *Groups that have open-mindedness norms:* R. Mitchell, B. Boyle, and S. Nicolas, "The Impact of Goal Structure in Team Knowledge Creation," *Group Processes & Intergroup Relations* 12, no. 5 (2009): 639–651.

Chapter 4

83. *The relationship the leaders had:* H. Liao, D. Liu, and R. Loi, "Looking at Both Sides of the Social Exchange Coin: A Social Cognitive Perspective on the Joint Effects of Relationship Quality and Differentiation on Creativity," *Academy of Management Journal* 53, no. 5 (2010): 1090–1109.

83. *What's more, those who solicit:* K. Stobbeleier, S. Ashford, and D. Buyens, "Self-Regulation of Creativity at Work: The Role of Feedback-Seeking Behavior in Creative Performance," *Academy of Management Journal,* 54, no. 4 (2011): 811–831.

84. *Managers have reported cases:* R. Alsop, *The Trophy Kids Grow Up: How the Millennial Generation Is Shaking Up the Workplace* (San Francisco: Jossey-Bass, 2008).

84. *In a study that compared the impact:* C.E. Shalley and J.E. Perry-Smith, "Effects of Social-Psychological Factors on Creative Performance: The Role of Informational and Controlling Expected Evaluation and Modeling Experience," *Organizational Behavior and Human Decision Processes* 84, no. 1 (2001): 1–22.

85. *Excellent leaders offer developmental feedback:* J.M. George and J. Zhou, "Dual Tuning in a Supportive Context: Joint Contributions of Positive Mood, Negative Mood, and Supervisory Behaviors to Employee Creativity," *Academy of Management Journal* 50, no. 3 (2007): 605–622.

86. *Excellent leaders display interactional justice:* Ibid.

86. *For example, a study of creativity:* J. Zhou and J.M. George, "When Job Dissatisfaction Leads to Creativity: Encouraging the Expression of Voice," *Academy of Management Journal* 44, no. 4), 682–696.

86. *Excellent leaders are trustworthy:* Ibid.

87. *It took another five years to perfect:* Lemelson-MIT, "Inventor of the Week: Art Fry and Spencer Silver, Post-it Notes," Massachusetts Institute of Technology, www.mit.edu.

87. *The ambidextrous leader switches:* K. Rosing, M. Frese, and A. Bausch, "Explaining the Heterogeneity of the Leadership-Innovation Relationship: Ambidextrous Leadership," *Leadership Quarterly* 22 (2011): 956–974.

87. *They make investments in people:* B.J. Avolio, B.M. Bass, and D. Jung, "Reexamining the Components of Transformational and

Transactional Leadership Using the Multifactor Leadership Questionnaire," *Journal of Occupational and Organizational Psychology* 7 (1999): 441–462.

88. *Conversely, transformational leaders:* B.M. Bass, *Leadership and Performance Beyond Expectations* (New York: Free Press, 1985).

88. *Transformational leaders are more likely:* Y. Gong, J.C. Huang, and J.L. Farh, "Employee Learning Orientation, Transformational Leadership, and Employee Creativity: The Mediating Role of Employee Creative Self-Efficacy," *Academy of Management Journal* 52, no. 4 (2009):, 765–778; L. Gumusluoglu and A. Ilsev, "Transformational Leadership, Creativity, and Organizational Innovation," *Journal of Business Research* 62, no. 4 (2009): 461–473.

88. *The positive relationship:* S.O. Cheung, P.S.P. Wong, and A.W.Y. Wu, "Towards an Organizational Culture Framework in Construction," *International Journal of Project Management* 29, no. 1 (2011): 33–44.

88. *Similar positive results:* Gumusluoglu and Ilsev, "Leadership, Creativity, and Organizational Innovation."

88. *Transformational leadership also is related to increased creativity:* S.J. Shin and J. Zhou, "Transformational Leadership, Conservation, and Creativity: Evidence from Korea," *Academy of Management Journal* 46, no. 6 (2003): 703–714.

89. *Powerful people generate:* A.D. Galinsky, J.C. Magee, D.H. Gruenfeld, J.A. Whitson, and K.A. Lilenquist, "Power Reduces the Press of the Situation: Implications for Creativity, Conformity and Dissonance," *Journal of Personality and Social Psychology* 95, no. 6 (2008): 1450–1466.

91. *When leaders are verbally dominant:* L. Tost, F. Gino, and R. Larrick, "When Power Makes Others Speechless: The Negative Impact of Leader Power on Team Performance" (working paper, 2011).

91. *Creative deviance refers to:* C. Mainemelis, "Stealing Fire: Creative Deviance in the Evolution of New Ideas," *Academy of Management Review* 35, no. 4 (2010): 558–578.

91. *The Pontiac Fiero:* G. Pinchot, III, *Intrapreneuring* (New York: Harper & Row, 1985).

91. *The film* The Godfather *was born:* J. Lewis, "If History Has Taught Us Anything . . . " Francis Ford Coppola, Paramount Pictures, and *The Godfather, Parts I, II, III*," in *Francis Ford Coppola's The Godfather Trilogy*, ed. N. Browne (Cambridge: Cambridge University Press J. (2000), 23–56.

92. *Churchill recognized:* J.R.P. French and B.H. Raven, "The Bases of Social Power," in *Group Dynamics*, ed. D. Cartwright and A.F. Zander (New York: Harper & Row, 1968), 259–270.

Chapter 5

96. *However, there is an ego-driven:* C. Heath, "On the Social Psychology of Agency Relationships: Lay Theories of Motivation Overemphasize Extrinsic Rewards," *Organizational Behavior and Human Decision Processes* 78, no. 1 (1999): 25–62.

98. *The message: find a way:* M. Vansteenkiste, J. Simons, W. Lens, K. Sheldon, and E. Deci, "Motivating Learning, Performance, and Persistence: The Synergistic Effect of Intrinsic Goal Contents and Autonomy-Supported Contexts," *Journal of Personality and Social Psychology* 87, no. 2 (2004): 246–260.

98. *By coming to such a conclusion:* L. Festinger and J.M. Carlsmith, "Cognitive Consequences of Forced Compliance," *Journal of Abnormal and Social Psychology* 58 (1955): 203–210.

99. *And indeed, the least creative projects:* T.M. Amabile, "Motivational Synergy: Toward New Conceptualizations of Intrinsic and Extrinsic Motivation in the Workplace," *Human Resource Management Review* 3, no. 3 (1993): 185–201; T.M. Amabile, E. Phillips, and M.A. Collins, "Personality and Environmental Determinants of Creativity in Professional Artists," (unpublished manuscript, Brandeis University, Waltham, MA, 1993).

99. *Employees' expected reward:* R. Eisenberger and J. Aselage, "Incremental Effects of Reward on Experienced Performance Pressure: Positive Outcomes for Intrinsic Interest and Creativity," *Journal of Organizational Behavior* 30, no. 1 (2009): 95–117.

99. *Performance pressure increases intrinsic interest:* Ibid.

99. *People who receive rewards:* Ibid.

99. *Indeed, when youngsters are given:* R. Eisenberger and L. Rhoades, "Incremental Effects of Reward on Creativity," *Journal of Personality and Social Psychology* 81, no. 4 (2001): 728–741; R. Eisenberger, F. Haskins, and P. Gambleton, "Promised Reward and Creativity: Effects of Prior Experience," *Journal of Experimental Social Psychology* 35, no. 3 (1999): 308–325.

100. *This reward-creativity relationship:* R. Eisenberger, S. Armeli, and J. Pretz, "Can the Promise of Reward Increase Creativity?" *Journal of Personality and Social Psychology* 74, no. 3 (1998): 704–714.

100. *Reward promised for creativity:* Eisenberger and Rhoades, "Incremental Effects of Reward on Creativity."

100. *Employees who expected to be rewarded:* Ibid.

101. *Also, children praised for intelligence:* C.M. Mueller and C.S. Dweck, "Praise for Intelligence Can Undermine Children's Motivation and Performance," *Journal of Personality and Social Psychology* 75, no. 1 (1998): 33–52.

101. *Those who had engaged in the creative pre-task:* R. Conti, T.M. Amabile, and S. Pollak, "The Positive Impact of Creative Activity: Effects of Creative Task Engagement and Motivational Focus on College Students' Learning," *Personality and Social Psychology Bulletin* 21, no. 10 (1995): 1107–1116.

101. *Most important, they have struck a balance:* M. Csikszentmihalyi, *Flow: The Psychology of Optimal Experience* (New York: Harper & Row, 1990).

102. *Football analyst and former coach:* B. Gumbel, *Real Sports with Byant Gumbel*, episode 185, August 21, 2012.

102. *The team tested everything:* N. Peck, "Charter House Innovations' Audacious Goals Let Design Team Flex Creative Muscles," MiBiz. com, December 20, 2010.

103. *Because the software immediately translates:* P. Wolfson, "UMd. Team Changes Lives with Treadmill and a Webcam," *WTOP*, June 25, 2012, wtop.com.

103. *To limit the distractions:* R. Vesely, "Social Life, Not Social Media, Is Work's Biggest Distraction," *Workforce*, June 27, 2012, workforce.com.

103. *Page says that having meetings go longer:* C. Miller, "Google's Chief Works to Trim a Bloated Ship," *New York Times*, November 9, 2001, nytimes.com.

104. *Tellingly, their coach explains:* J. Yuan, "Olympics Prime-time Recap: So Many Greatest-Evers," nymag.com, August 10, 2012.

104. *Later, when all the children:* Mueller and Dweck, "Praise for Intelligence Can Undermine Children's Motivation and Performance."

104. *Similarly, another investigation revealed:* M.A. Finkelstein, "Intrinsic Versus Extrinsic Motivational Orientations and the Volunteer Process," *Personality and Individual Differences* 46 (2009): 653–658.

105. *Inspiration is a motivational state:* T.M. Thrash, L.A. Maruskin, S.E. Cassidy, J.W. Fryer, and R.M. Ryan, "Mediating Between the Muse and the Masses: Inspiration and the Actualization of Creative Ideas," *Journal of Personality and Social Psychology* 98, no. 3 (2010): 469–487.

105. *Those who had written:* T.M. Thrash and A.J. Elliott, "Inspiration: Core Characteristics, Component Processes, Antecedents, and Function," *Journal of Personality and Social Psychology* 87, no. 6 (2004): 957–973.

106. *At first, she started making a few balloons:* M. Warren, "After a Bad Accident, Finding Resilience in Balloons," *New York Times*, November 7, 2001.

106. *In one investigation, the highest level:* C.E. Shalley, "Effects of Coaction, Expected Evaluation, and Goal Setting on Creativity and Productivity," *Academy of Management Journal* 38, no. 2 (1995): 483–503.

106. *Those who were shown the photo:* A. Shantz and G. Latham, "An Exploratory Field Experiment of the Effect of Subconscious and Conscious Goals on Employee Performance," *Organizational Behavior and Human Decision Processes* 109, no. 1 (2009): 9–17.

106. *Another study indicated that people:* Ibid.

107. *Participants in both the diet and the food:* A. Fishbach, R. Friedman, and A. Kruglanski, "Leading Us Not into Temptation: Momentary Allurements Elicit Overriding Goal Activation," *Journal of Personality and Social Psychology* 84, no. 2 (2003): 296–309.

107. *One investigation of female engineers:* C.Y. Cheng, J. Sanchez-Burks, and F. Lee, "Connecting the Dots Within: Creative Performance and Identity Integration." *Psychological Science* 19, no. 11 (2008): 1178–1184.

107. *Indeed, there is a strong, positive linear relationship:* M.A. Davis, "Understanding the Relationship Between Mood and Creativity: A Meta-Analysis," *Organizational Behavior and Human Decision Processes* 108, no. 1 (2009): 25–38; M.J. Grawitch, D.C. Munz, and T.J. Kramer, "Effects of Member Mood States on Creative Performance in Temporary Workgroups," *Group Dynamics: Theory, Research, and Practice* 7, no. 1 (2003): 41–54; T.M. Amabile, S.G. Barsade, J.S. Mueller, and B.M. Staw, "Affect and Creativity at Work," *Administrative Science Quarterly* 50, no. 3 (2005): 367–403; A.M. Isen, K.A. Daubman, and G.P. Nowicki, "Positive Affect Facilitates Creative Problem Solving," *Journal of Personality and Social Psychology* 47 (1987): 1026–1217.

108. *Perhaps the most persuasive evidence:* M.A. Davis, "Understanding the Relationship Between Mood and Creativity: A Meta-Analysis," *Organizational Behavior and Human Decision Processes* 108, no. 1 (2009): 25–38.

108. *In short, unhappy leaders:* C. Anderson and L.L. Thompson, "Affect from the Top Down: How Powerful Individuals' Positive Affect Shapes Negotiations," *Organizational Behavior and Human Decision Processes* 95 (2003): 125–139.

109. *As a start, he used:* G. Burnison, "Learning the Softer Side of Leadership," *Fast Company*, March 13, 2012, fastcompany.com.

109. *Indeed, people who witness:* C.L. Poratha and A. Erez, "Overlooked but Not Untouched: How Rudeness Reduces Onlookers' Performance on Routine and Creative Tasks," *Organizational Behavior and Human Decision Processes* 109, no. 1 (2009): 29–44.

109. *And unbridled anger:* C. Scheinbaum, "Doctors Without Boundaries," *Bloomberg Businessweek*, August 6, 2012.

109. *Positive affect is a precursor:* Amabile et al., "Affect and Creativity at Work."

109. *In another investigation, temporary workgroups:* Grawitch, Munz, and Kramer, "Effects of Member Mood States on Creative Performance in Temporary Workgroups."

109. *People who are led:* M.J. Grawitch, D.C. Munz, E.K. Elliott, and A. Mathis, "Promoting Creativity in Temporary Problem-Solving Groups: The Effects of Positive Mood and Autonomy in Problem Definition on Idea-Generating Performance," *Group Dynamics: Theory, Research, and Practice* 7, no. 3 (2003): 200–213.

109. *Similarly, people who have been offered:* W.M.P. Klein, "Effects of Objective Feedback and 'Single Other' or 'Average Other' Social Comparison Feedback on Performance Judgments and Helping Behavior," *Personality and Social Psychology Bulletin*, 29, no. 3 (2003): 418–429.

109. *Yet, does negative mood always:* E.E. Jones and J.R. Kelly, "No Pain, No Gains: Negative Mood Leads to Process Gains in Idea-Generation Groups," *Group Dynamics* 13, no. 2 (2009): 75–88.

109. *For example, groups of people:* Ibid.

110. *And positive mood may not help:* R.J. Melton, "The Role of Positive Affect in Syllogism Performance," *Personality and Social Psychology Bulletin* 1 (1995): 788–794.

110. *For example, people in positive moods:* Ibid.

110. *A study of feigned affect:* M. Sliter, S. Jex, K. Wolford, and J. McInnerney, "How Rude! Emotional Labor as a Mediator Between Customer Incivility and Employee Outcomes," *Journal of Occupational Health Psychology* 15 (2010): 468–481.

110. *Psychologists refer to this:* R. B. Zajonc, "Mere Exposure: A Gateway to the Subliminal," *Current Directions in Psychological Science* 10, no. 6 (December 2011).

111. *Happy people effectively transform:* E.R. Hirt, E.E. Devers, and S.M. McCrea, "I Want to Be Creative: Exploring the Role of Hedonic Contingency Theory in the Positive Mood-Cognitive Flexibility Link," *Journal of Personality and Social Psychology* 94, no. 2 (2008): 214–230.

111. *Activating moods lead:* C.K.W. De Dreu and B.A. Nijstad, "Mental Set and Creative Thought in Social Conflict: Threat Rigidity Versus Motivated Focus," *Journal of Personality and Social Psychology* 95, no. 3 (2008): 648–661.

111. *The reason negative activating moods:* B.A. Nijstad, C.K.W. DeDreu, E.F. Rietzschel, and M. Baas, "The Dual Pathway to Creativity Model. Creative Ideation as a Function of Flexibility and Persistence," *European Review of Social Psychology* 21 (2010): 34–77.

112. *Men who sat more:* A.V. Patel and L. Bernstein, "Leisure Time Spent Sitting in Relation to Total Mortality in a Prospective Cohort of US Adults," *American Journal of Epidemiology* 172, no. 4 (2010): 419–429.

112. *Keith Rabois, COO of Square:* J. Guynn, "Silicon Valley Is Getting Healthy: Crunching Abs, Not Just Apps," May 11, 2012, latimes.com.

112. *My colleagues and I:* B. Lucas and L. Thompson, "The Problem with "Don't Worry, Be Happy" (manuscript in preparation, Kellogg School of Management, 2013).

112. *Negative moods can increase creativity:* J.M. George and J. Zhou, "Dual Tuning in a Supportive Context: Joint Contributions of Positive Mood, Negative Mood, and Supervisory Behaviors to Employee Creativity," *Academy of Management Journal* 50, no. 3 (2007): 605–622.

113. *Executives who shared embarrassing stories:* B. Lucas and L. Thompson, "The Problem with "Don't Worry, Be Happy" (Kellogg School of Management, forthcoming 2013).

115. *Similarly, most people feel:* M. E. P. Seligman, *Authentic Happiness* (New York: Free Press, 2002), p. 15.

115. *Another widely researched measure:* S. Lyubomirsky and H.S. Lepper, "A Measure of Subjective Happiness: Preliminary Reliability and Construct Validation," *Social Indicators Research* 46 (1999): 137–155.

116. *The positive effects:* M.E.P. Seligman, "Foreword: The Past and Future of Positive Psychology," in *Flourishing: Positive Psychology and the Life Well Lived*, ed. C.L.M. Keyes and J. Haidt (Washington, DC: American Psychological Association, 2003): xi–xx.

116. *Bottom line: improving:* M. Seligman, "Authentic Happiness: Using the New Positive Psychology to Realize Your Potential for Lasting Fulfillment (New York: Free Press/Simon & Schuster, 2002): 9.

117. *A study of twenty-two lottery winners:* P. Brickman, D. Coates, and R. Janoff-Bulman, "Lottery Winners and Accident Victims: Is Happiness Relative?" *Journal of Personality and Social Psychology* 36, no. 8 (1978): 917–927.

117. *These effects last:* E. Pronin and D.M. Wegner, "Manic Thinking: Independent Effects of Thought Speed and Thought Content on Mood," *Psychological Science* 17 (2006): 807–813; S. Lyubomirsky, *The How of Happiness: A Scientific Approach to Getting the Life You Want* (New York: Penguin Press, 2008); M. Mehl et al. "Eavesdropping on Happiness: Well-Being Is Related to Having Less Small Talk and More Substantive Conversations," *Psychological Science* 21, no. 4 (2010): 539–541.

117. *People who have a deep, meaningful conversation:* M. Mehl et al., "Eavesdropping on Happiness: Well-being Is Related to Having Less Small Talk and More Substantive Conversations," *Psychological Science,* 2010.

118. *Rapidly and energetically:* E. Pronin and D.M. Wegner, (2006). "Manic Thinking: Independent Effects of Thought Speed and Thought Content on Mood," *Psychological Science* 17 (2006): 807–813.

118. *People who brainstorm:* S. Lyubomirsky, *The How of Happiness: A Scientific Approach to Getting the Life You Want* (New York: Penguin Press, 2008).

Chapter 6

121. *However, he self-silenced because:* "Bono's Take on Spider-Man," *The Week,* July 1–8, 2011, 8.

122. *They fight fairly:* J.M. Gottman and C.I. Notarius, "Decade Review: Observing Marital Interaction," *Journal of Marriage and the Family* 62 (2000): 927–947.

123. *In this case, teams composed:* See W.R. Fry, I. Firestone, and D. Williams, "Negotiation Process and Outcome of Stranger Dyads and Dating Couples: Do Lovers Lose?" *Basic and Applied Social Psychology* 4 (1983): 1–16; L. Thompson and T. DeHarpport, "Social Judgment, Feedback, and Interpersonal Learning in Negotiation," *Organizational Behavior and Human Decision Process* 58 (1994): 327–45.

123. In contrast, *relationship conflict:* J.L. Farh, C. Lee, and C.I. Farh, "Task Conflict and Team Creativity: A Question of How Much and When," *Journal of Applied Psychology* 95, no. 6 (2010):1173–1180.

124. *As it turned out, the men who:* R.I. Swaab and D.F. Swaab, "Sex Differences in the Effects of Visual Contact and Eye Contact in Negotiations," *Journal of Experimental Social Psychology* 45, no. 1 (2009): 129–136.

126. *According to Kellogg professor Vicki Medvec:* L. Van Boven, G. Thomas, and V.H. Medvec, "The Illusion of Transparency in Negotiations," *Negotiation Journal* 19, no. 2 (2003): 117–131.

127. *According to Harvey:* J. Harvey, "The Abilene Paradox: The Management of Agreement," *Organizational Dynamics* 3, no. 1 (1974): 63–80.

128. *In a six-person group:* M.E. Shaw, *Group Dynamics: The Psychology of Small Group Behavior,* 3rd ed. (New York: McGraw-Hill, 1981), 170.

129. *Groups that use brainwriting:* P.B. Paulus and H. Yang, "Idea Generation in Groups: A Basis for Creativity in Organizations," *Organizational Behavior and Human Decision Processes* 82, no. 1 (2000): 76–87; A.F. Osborn, *Applied Imagination,* 3rd ed. (New York: Scribner, 1993).

130. *Brainwriting can be made:* Paulus and Yang, "Idea Generation in Groups."

131. *The research findings overwhelmingly indicate:* S. Kavadias and S.C. Sommer, "The Effects of Problem Structure and Team Diversity on Brainstorming Effectiveness," *Management Science* 5, no. 12 (2009): 1899–1913.

131. *Not only do nominal groups outperform:* C. Faure, "Beyond Brainstorming: Effects of Different Group Procedures on Selection of Ideas and Satisfaction with the Process," *Journal of Creative Behavior* 38, no. 1 (2004): 13–34.

131. *This question was further examined:* V.L. Putman and P.B. Paulus, "Brainstorming, Brainstorming Rules and Decision Making," *Journal of Creative Behavior* 43, no. 1 (2009): 23–39.

132. *There is some evidence:* W.H. Cooper, R.B. Gallupe, S. Pollard, and J. Cadsby, "Some Liberating Effects of Anonymous Electronic Brainstorming," *Small Group Research* 29, no. 2 (1998):147–178.

132. *Moreover, anonymous:* Ibid.

132. *Groups using electronic brainstorming:* M. Nagasundaram and A.R. Dennis, "When a Group Is Not a Group: The Cognitive Foundation of Group Idea Generation," *Small Group Research* 24, no. 4 (1993): 463–489.

132. *One investigation compared the quality:* H. Barki and A. Pinsonneault, "Small Group Brainstorming and Idea Quality: Is Electronic Brainstorming the Most Effective Approach?" *Small Group Research* 32, no. 2 (2001): 158–205.

132. *The electronic brainstorming application:* O. Hilliges, L. Terrenghi, S. Boring, J. Kim, H. Richter, and A. Butz, "Designing for Collaborative Creative Problem Solving," *Creativity and Cognition* (2007): 137–146.

133. *Brainstorming groups and nominal groups:* M.W. Kramer, C.L. Kuo, and J.C. Dailey, "The Impact of Brainstorming Techniques on Subsequent Group Processes: Beyond Generating Ideas," *Small Group Research*, 28, no. 2 (1997): 218–242.

135. *In 2005, Mark Lucovsky:* I. Fried, "Court Docs: Ballmer Vowed to 'Kill' Google," *CNET News*, September 5, 2005, http://news.cnet.com.

135. *Another example of malignant conflict:* "The Wisconsin Judge Accused of Choking a Colleague," *The Week*, June 11, 2011, theweek.com.

136. *According to George Anderson:* C. Scheinbaum, "Doctors without Boundaries: An Anger Management Pioneer Tries to Defuse Rageaholic Physicians," *Bloomberg Businessweek*, August 6–12, 2012, 67–69.

136. *Jeer pressure:* L.M. Janes and J.M. Olson, "Jeer Pressure: The Behavioral Effects of Observing Ridicule of Others," *Personality and Social Psychology Bulletin* 26, no. 4 (2000): 474–485.

136. *In short, jeer pressure:* Ibid.

136. *In one investigation, top management teams:* S. Parayitam and R.S. Dooley, "Is Too Much Cognitive Conflict in Strategic Decision-Making Teams Too Bad?" *International Journal of Conflict Management* 22, no. 4 (2011): 342–357.

137. *As it turns out, debate:* C.J. Nemeth, B. Personnaz, M. Personnaz, and J.A. Goncalo, "The Liberating Role of Conflict in Group Creativity: A Study in Two Countries," *European Journal of Social Psychology* 34, no. 4 (2004): 365–374.

137. *Debate instructions were superior:* Ibid.

137. *Conversely, teams that engage:* L. Lu, F. Zhou, and K. Leung, "Effects of Task and Relationship Conflict on Individual Work Behaviors," *International Journal of Conflict Management* 22, no. 2 (2009): 131–150.

138. *My colleagues:* J.B. White, R.O. Tynan, A.D. Galinsky, and L. Thompson, "Face Threat Sensitivity in Negotiation: Roadblock to Agreement and Joint Gain," *OBHDP* 94 (2004): 102–124.

138. *Those who had read the "we" paragraph:* E. Seeley, W. Gardner, and L. Thompson, "The Role of the Self-Concept and the Social Context in Determining the Behavior of Power Holders: Self-Construal in Intergroup versus Dyadic Dispute Resolution Negotiations," *Journal of Personality and Social Psychology* 93, no. 4 (2007): 614–631.

140. *Of the four following behaviors:* See also C. Rusbult, N.A. Yovetich, and L. Verette, "An Interdependence Analysis of Accommodation Processes," in *Knowledge Structures in Close Relationships: A Social Psychological Approach*, ed. G.J.O. Fletcher and J. Fitness (Mahwah, NJ: Lawrence Erlbaum, 1996).

141. *If you suppress conflict:* C.K.W. De Dreu, D. Van Dierendonck, and M.T.M. Dijkstra, "Conflict at Work and Individual Well-Being," *International Journal of Conflict Management* 15, no. 1 (2004): 6–26.

145. *After receiving a heavy dose:* L. Babauta, "How to Accept Criticism with Grace and Appreciation," *Zenhabits*, 2012. Zenhabits.net.

146. *But I think the main thing is:* C.S. Einhorn, "Do Better CEOs Get Better Feedback?" May 17, 2012, chiefexecutive.net.

147. *Conversely, respect is:* R.C. Mayer, J.H. Davis, and F.D. Schoorman, "An Integrative Model of Organization Trust," *Academy of Management* 2, no. 3 (1995): 709–734; M.A. Cronin and L.R.Weingart, "The Differential Effects of Trust and Respect on Team Conflict," in *Conflict in Organizational Groups*, ed. L. Thompson and K.J. Behfar (Evanston, IL: Northeastern University Press, 2007).

147. *To measure the amount of trust:* Cronin and Weingart, "The Differential Effects of Trust and Respect on Team Conflict."

147. *To assess the amount of respect:* Ibid.

149. *People in teams size up:* A. Edmondson, "Psychological Safety and Learning Behavior in Work Teams," *Administrative Science Quarterly* 44 (1999): 350–383.

149. *Thus, even though people:* J. Mayer and T. Mussweiler, "Suspicious Spirits, Flexible Minds: When Distrust Enhances Creativity," *Journal of Personality and Social Psychology* 101, no. 6 (2011): 1262–1277.

Chapter 7

155. *Groups benefit best from building:* N.W. Kohn, P.B. Paulus, and Y.H. Choi, "Building on the Ideas of Others: An Examination of the Idea Combination Process," *Journal of Experimental Social Psychology* 47, no. 3 (2011): 554–561.

155. *Indeed, the scientific evidence:* E.H. Witte, "Toward Group Facilitation Technique for Project Teams," *Group Processes and Intergroup Relations* 10 (2007): 299–309.

155. *Brainstorming rules alone:* R.C. Litchfield, "Brainstorming Rules as Assigned Goals: Does Brainstorming Really Improve Idea Quantity?" *Motivation and Emotion* 33, no. 1 (2009): 25–31.

156. *They coached some groups:* P.B. Paulus, T. Nakui, V.L. Putman, and V.R. Brown, "Effects of Task Instructions and Brief Breaks on Brainstorming," *Group Dynamics* 10, no. 3 (2006): 206–219.

157. *Groups with a facilitator:* A.K. Offner, T.J. Kramer, and J.P. Winter, "The Effects of Facilitation, Recording, and Pauses on Group Brainstorming," *Small Group Research* 27, no. 2 (1996): 283–298.

157. *And face-to-face groups:* T.J. Kramer, G.P. Fleming, and S.M. Mannis, "Improving Face-to-Face Brainstorming Through Modeling and Facilitation," *Small Group Research* 32, no. 5 (2001): 533–557.

157. *Those given the quantity goal:* P.B. Paulus, D.W. Kohn, and L.E. Arditti, "Effects of Quantity and Quality Instructions on Brainstorming," *Journal of Creative Behavior* 45, no. 1 (2011), 38–46.

158. *Indeed, the productivity gap:* P.B. Paulus and M.T. Dzindolet, "Social Influence Processes in Group Brainstorming," *Journal of Personality and Social Psychology* 64, no. 4 (1993): 575–586.

158. *Novelty goals did not simply:* R.C. Litchfield, J. Fan, and V.R. Brown, "Directing Idea Generation Using Brainstorming with Specific Novelty Goals," *Motivation and Emotion* 35, no. 2 (2011): 135–140.

158. *Training had a significant:* J. Baruah and P.B. Paulus, "Effects of Training on Idea Generation in Groups," *Small Group Research* 39, no. 5 (2008): 523–541.

159. *The groups who learned brainstorming:* M.M. Casanoves, F. Miralles, M. Gomez, and R. Garcia, "Improving Creativity Results and Its Implementation in Organizations Using Creative Techniques Through Experimental Learning Training" *Proceedings of the 5th European Conference on Innovation and Entrepreneurship* (2010): 121–128.

159. *The group that warmed up:* H. Coşkun, "Close Associations and Memory in Brainwriting Groups, *Journal of Creative Behavior* 45, no. 1 (2011): 59–75.

159. *For most people, idea selection:* E.F. Rietzschel, B.A. Nijstad, and W. Stroebe, "Productivity Is Not Enough: A Comparison of Interactive and Nominal Brainstorming Groups on Idea Generation and Selection," *Journal of Experimental Social Psychology* 42, no. 2 (2006): 244–251.

159. *Not surprisingly, when people:* E.F. Rietzschel, B.A. Nijstad, and W. Stroebe, "The Selection of Creative Ideas After Individual Idea Generation: Choosing Between Creativity and Impact," *British Journal of Psychology 101* (2010): 47–68.

160. *In fact, if anything, nominal groups:* V.L. Putman and P.B. Paulus, "Brainstorming, Brainstorming Rules, and Decision Making," *Journal of Creative Behavior* 43, no. 1 (2009): 23–39; C. Faure, "Beyond Brainstorming: Effects of Different Group Procedures on Selection of Ideas and Satisfaction with the Process," *Journal of Creative Behavior* 38, no. 1 (2004): 13–34.

160. *In another investigation:* Rietzschel, Nijstad, and Stroebe, "Productivity Is Not Enough."

160. *Indeed, when people feel uncertain:* S. Jennifer, J. Mueller, S. Melwani, and J. Goncalo, "The Bias Against Creativity: Why People Desire but Reject Creative Ideas," *Psychological Science* 23, no. 1 (2012): 13–17.

160. *Similarly, solitary idea generation:* Baruah and Paulus, "Effects of Training on Idea Generation in Groups."

161. *Indeed, groups organized with:* K. Girotra, C. Terwiesch, and K.T. Ulrich, "Idea Generation and the Quality of the Best Idea," *Management Science* 56, no. 4 (2010): 591–605.

161. *In one set of intriguing experiments:* Ibid.

161. *If this does happen, don't fear:* N.W. Kohn and S.M. Smith, "Collaborative Fixation: Effects of Others' Ideas on Brainstorming," *Applied Cognitive Psychology* 25, no. 3 (2011): 359–371.

161. *So my colleague, Hoon-Seok Choi:* H-S. Choi and L. Thompson, "Old Wine in New Bottles: Impact on Membership Change of Group Creativity," *Organizational Behavior and Human Decision Process* 98, no. 2 (2005):121–132.

163. *As they work together*: L.L. Thompson and T.R. Cohen, "Metacognition in Teams and Organizations," in *Social Metacognition*, ed. P. Brinol and K.G. DeMarree (New York: Psychology Press, 2011).

163. *Unfortunately, team mental models*: P.F. Skilton and K.J. Dooley, "The Effects of Repeat Collaboration on Creative Abrasion," *Academy of Management Review* 35, no. 1 (2010): 118–134.

163. *The diversity of the team*: R. Haykin, "Creative Abrasion vs. Creative Collaboration," *Innovation Sparks*, October 2, 2009, haykin.net.

163. *Cirque du Soleil CEO Daniel Lamarre*: A. Dan, "The Secret That Inspires Cirque du Soleil's Culture of Innovation: Creative Friction," *Forbes*. May 29, 2012, www.forbes.com.

164. *For closed groups*: M. Baer, R.T.A.J. Leenders, G.R. Oldham, and A.K. Vadera, "Win or Lose the Battle for Creativity: The Power and Perils of Intergroup Competition," *Academy of Management Journal* 53, no. 4 (2010): 827–845.

164. *Groups using serial mode*: G.J. DeVreede, R.O. Briggs, and R. Reiter-Palmon, "Exploring Asynchronous Brainstorming in Large Groups: A Field Comparison of Serial and Parallel Subgroups," *Human Factor*, 52, no. 2 (2010): 189–202.

164. *In one investigation, people were asked*: D.L. Zabelina and M.D. Robinson, "Child's Play: Facilitating the Originality of Creative Output by a Priming Manipulation," *Psychology of Aesthetics, Creativity, and the Arts* 4, no. 1 (2010): 57–65.

165. *Dissent, debate, and competing views*: C.J. Nemeth, B. Personnaz, M. Personnaz, and J.A. Goncalo, "The Liberating Role of Conflict in Group Creativity: A Study in Two Countries," *European Journal of Social Psychology* 34, no. 4 (2004): 365–374.

166. *In other words, granting*: Ibid.

166. *Moreover, group members are*: L. Troyer and R. Youngreen, "Conflict and Creativity in Groups," *Journal of Social Issues* 65, no. 2 (2009): 409–427.

166. *These hours are just perfect*: E. Miron-Spektor, D. Efrat-Treister, A. Rafaeli, and O. Schwarz-Cohen, "Others' Anger Makes People Work Harder, Not Smarter: The Effect of Observing Anger and Sarcasm on Creative and Analytic Thinking," *Journal of Applied Psychology* 96, no. 5 (2011): 1065–1075.

167. *The students who were given*: H. Coşkun, P.B. Paulus, V. Brown, and J.J. Sherwood, "Cognitive Stimulation and Problem Presentation in Idea-Generating Groups," *Group Dynamics: Theory, Research, and Practice* 4, no. 4 (2000), 307–329.

167. *For example, one study examined:* T.J. Howard, E.A. Dekonick, and S.J. Culley, "The Use of Creative Stimuli at Early Stages of Product Innovation," *Research in Engineering Design* 21, no. 4 (2010): 263–274.

168. *All these trappings:* J. Eells, "Jack Outside the Box," *New York Times*, April 5, 2012, nytimes.com.

168. *For example, in one investigation:* K.L. Dugosh, P.B. Paulus, E.J. Roland, and H.C. Yang, "Cognitive Stimulation in Brainstorming," *Journal of Personality and Social Psychology* 79, no. 5 (2000): 722–735.

168. *In fact, groups given an opportunity:* R. Ziegler, M. Diehl, and G. Zijlstra, "Idea Production in Nominal and Virtual Groups: Does Computer-Mediated Communication Improve Group Brainstorming?" *Group Processes and Intergroup Relations* 3, no. 2 (2000): 141–158.

168. *Exposing people to stimulus:* B.A. Nijstad, W. Stroebe, and H.F.M. Lodewijkx, "Cognitive Stimulation and Interference in Groups: Exposure Effects in an Idea Generation Task," *Journal of Experimental Social Psychology* 38, no. 6 (2002): 535–544.

168. *The creative example was the most effective:* C.E. Shalley and J.E. Perry-Smith, "Effects of Social-Psychological Factors on Creative Performance: The Role of Informational and Controlling Expected Evaluation and Modeling Experience," *Organizational Behavior and Human Decision Processes* 84, no. 1 (2001): 1–22.

168. *A study by Hamit Coşkun:* H. Coşkun, "Cognitive Stimulation with Convergent and Divergent Thinking Exercises in Brainwriting: Incubation, Sequence Priming, and Group Context," *Small Group Research* 36, no. 4 (2005): 466–498.

169. *Similarly, divergent thinking:* H. Coşkun, "The Effects of Associate Exercises on the Idea Generation During Brainstorming," *Turkish Journal of Psychology* 24, no. 64 (2009): 34–46.

169. *People in one study went:* E.F. Rietzschel, B.A. Nijstad, and W. Stroebe, "Relative Accessibility of Domain Knowledge and Creativity: The Effects of Knowledge Activation on the Quantity and Originality of Generated Ideas," *Journal of Experimental Social Psychology* 43, no. 6 (2007): 933–946.

169. *Indeed, those who have lived abroad:* W.W. Maddux, H. Adam, and A.D. Galinsky, "When in Rome . . . Learn Why the Romans Do What They Do: How Multicultural Learning Experiences Facilitate Creativity, *Personality and Social Psychology Bulletin* 36, no. 6 (2010): 731–741.

170. *Even more disconcerting:* D.G. Ancona, G.A. Okhuysen, and L.A. Perlow, "Taking Time to Integrate Temporal Research," *Academy of Management Review* 26, (2001): 512–529.

170. *One investigation compared:* J.R. Kelly and S.J. Karau, "Entrainment of Creativity in Small Groups," *Small Group Research* 24, no. 2 (1993): 179–198.

170. *The point of this story:* George Washington University, Winston Lord China, National Security Archive [episode 15] (Washington DC: The George Washington University, January 24, 1999).

171. *Then, like speed dating:* C.K. Joyce, K.E. Jennings, J. Hey, J.C. Grossman, and T. Kalil, "Getting Down to Business: Using Speedstorming to Initiate Creative Cross-Disciplinary Collaboration," *Creativity and Innovation Management* 19, no. 1 (2010): 57–67.

172. *A direct comparison of speedstorming:* Ibid.

172. *The bigger the group:* B.A. Nijstad, W. Stroebe, and H.F.M. Lodewijkx, "Persistence Of Brainstorming Groups: How Do People Know When To Stop?" *Journal of Experimental Social Psychology* 35, no. 2 (1999): 165–185.

172. *Using insights from brain activation:* R.S. Friedman and J. Förster, "The Effects of Approach and Avoidance Motor Actions on the Elements of Creative Insight," *Journal of Personality and Social Psychology* 79, no. 4 (2000): 477–492.

172. *Note: they also found:* Ibid.

173. *A promotion focus:* R.S. Friedman and J. Förster, "The Effects of Promotion and Prevention Cues on Creativity," *Journal of Personality and Social Psychology* 81, no. 6 (2001): 1001–1013.

173. *It is worth noting:* M. Baas, C.K.W. DeDreu, and B. Nijstad, "When Prevention Promotes Creativity: The Role of Mood, Regulatory Focus and Regulatory Closure," *Journal of Personality and Social Psychology*, 100, no. 5 (2011): 794–809.

173. *Indeed, people who focus:* R.S. Friedman and J.Förster, "Effects of Motivational Cues on Perceptual Asymmetry: Implications for Creativity and Analytical Problem Solving," *Journal of Personality and Social Psychology* 88, no. 2 (2005): 263–275.

174. *Counter-factual thinking:* L.J. Kray, A.D. Galinsky, and E.M. Wong, "Thinking Within the Box: The Relational Processing Style Elicited by Counterfactual Mind-Sets," *Journal of Personality and Social Psychology* 91, no. 1 (2006): 33–48.

174. *One way of reversing the negative:* K.D. Markman, M.J. Lindberg, L.J. Kray, A.D. Galinsky, Implications of counterfactual structure for creative generation and analytical problem solving. *Personality and Social Psychology Bulletin* 33, no. 3 (2007): 312–324.

175. *And the data are clear:* N. Madjar, G.R. Oldham, and M.G. Pratt, "There's No Place Like Home? The Contributions of Work and Nonwork Creativity Support to Employees' Creative Performance," *Academy of Management Journal* 45, no. 4 (2002): 757–767.

175. *Indeed, when team managers:* M.R. Bashshur, A. Hernandez, and V. Gonzalez-Roma, "When Managers and Their Teams Disagree: A Longitudinal Look at the Consequences of Differences in Perceptions of Organizational Support," *Journal of Applied Psychology* 96, no. 3 (2011): 558–573.

175. *Samples of senior executives:* D.F. Caldwell and C.A. O'Reilly, "The Determinants of Team-Based Innovation in Organizations: The Role of Social Influence," *Small Group Research* 34, no. 4 (2003): 497–517.

175. *Of all of these, it is work-group:* T.C. DiLiello, J.D. Houghton, and D. Dawley, "Narrowing the Creativity Gap: The Moderating Effects of Perceived Support for Creativity," *Journal of Psychology* 145, no. 3 (2011): 151–172.

Chapter 8

181. *A field study of feedback-seeking:* S.J. Ashford and A.S. Tsui, "Self-Regulation for Managerial Effectiveness: the Role of Active Feedback Seeking," *Academy of Management Journal* 34, no. 2 (1991): 251–280.

183. *Remarkably, that seems to be true:* K.A. Ericsson, R.T. Krampe, and C. Tesch-Römer, "The Role of Deliberate Practice in the Acquisition of Expert Performance," *Psychological Review* 100, no. 3 (1993): 363–406.

184. *The biochemists had been trying:* D. Freeman, "Online Gamers Solve HIV Puzzle That Stymied Scientists," CBS News, Cbsnews.com.

185. *This is known as the inert knowledge problem:* L. Thompson, D. Gentner, and J. Lowenstein, "Avoiding Missed Opportunities in Managerial Life: Analogical Training More Powerful Than Individual Case Training," *Organizational Behavior and Human Decision Processes* 82 (2000): 60–75.

185. *Consider for example, the story of the general:* M.L. Gick and K.J. Holyoak, "Schema Introduction and Analogical Transfer," *Cognitive Psychology* 15 (1983): 1–38.

185. *A quite different problem is:* Ibid.

189. *Hirst found that teams:* G. Hirst, D. Van Knippenberg, and J. Zhou, "A Cross-Level Perspective on Employee Creativity: Goal Orientation, Team Learning Behavior, and Individual Creativity," *Academy of Management Journal* 52, 2 (2009): 280–293.

189. *For example, entrepreneurs construct meaning:* J.P. Cornelissen and J.S. Clarke, "Imagining and Rationalizing Opportunities: Inductive Reasoning and the Creation and Justification of New Ventures," *Academy of Management Review* 35, 4 (2010): 539–557.

189. *Rather, we found that the key:* D. Gentner, J. Loewenstein, L. Thompson, and K. Forbus, "Reviving Inert Knowledge: Analogical Encoding Supports Relational Retrieval of Past Events," *Cognitive Science* 33 (2009): 1343–1382; D. Gentner, J. Loewenstein, J. and L. Thompson,

"Learning and Transfer: A General Role for Analogical Encoding," *Journal of Educational Psychology* 95, no. 2 (2003): 393–408.

191. *Not surprisingly, they impact mood:* S.E. Taylor and J.D. Brown, "Illusion and Well-Being: A Social Psychological Perspective on Mental Health," *Psychological Bulletin* 103, no. 2 (1988): 193–210.

191. *This led to a self-fulfilling chain:* R. Rosenthal and L. Jacobson, "Teachers' Expectancies: Determinants of Pupils' IQ Gains," *Psychological Reports* 19 (1966): 115–118.

192. *The theory being tested:* M. Snyder, E.D. Tanke, and E. Berscheid, "Social Perception and Interpersonal Behavior: On the Self-Fulfilling Nature of Social Stereotypes," *Journal of Personality and Social Psychology* 35 (1977): 656–666.

192. *Perhaps it is for this reason:* P. Bierly, R.W. Kolodinsky, and B.J. Charette, "Understanding the Complex Relationship Between Creativity and Ethical Ideologies," *Journal of Business Ethics* 86 (1) (2009): 101–112.

193. *The data are in:* P.J. Silvia and A.G. Phillips, Self-Awareness, Self-Evaluation and Creativity, *Personality and Social Psychology Bulletin* 30, 8 (2004): 1009–1017.

193. *But what if the green room:* E.H. Schein, "How Can Organizations Learn Faster? The Challenge of Entering the Green Room," *Social Management Review* (1993): 85–92.

193. *According to management scientist guru:* Ibid.

INDEX

ABOUT THE AUTHOR

LEIGH THOMPSON is the J. Jay Gerber Professor of Dispute Resolution & Organizations at Northwestern University's Kellogg School of Management. She is the director of the Kellogg Team and Group Research Center, a research-based community of scholars dedicated to understanding and improving the performance of work teams in organizations. She also directs the Leading High Impact Teams executive program at Kellogg. An active scholar and researcher, Thompson has published more than 100 articles and chapters and has authored several books, including *The Mind and Heart of the Negotiator* (5th edition), *Making the Team* (4th edition), and *The Truth About Negotiations*.

Thompson's research focuses on team creativity, negotiation, and learning. Her most recent research projects include investigations of mood states and creativity, work ethic and team performance, and learning win-win negotiation skills.

Thompson has worked with private and public organizations in the United States, Latin America, Canada, Europe, and the Middle East. She serves on the editorial boards of several academic journals and is a member of the Academy of Management.

For more information about Leigh Thompson's teaching and research, please visit www.LeighThompson.com.